Essays in

Comparative Politics

Understanding Power and Global Political
Systems for AP Comparative Government

*A Student and Teacher Guide to Political Institutions,
Participation, and Change*

By Harold M. Hutchings

MR HUTCHINGS HISTORY

Published by Mr. Hutchings History
Under the T.W. Peterson & Sons imprint
Denver, Colorado
Founded 1947; honored in memoriam

First Edition
Printed in the United States of America

ISBN (Print): 979-8-9944293-0-3
ISBN (Digital): 979-8-9944293-1-0

Dedication

To Elaine, Henry, Zsa Zsa, and Spencer, for their support

Foreword

You are entering a field that asks big and important questions. Why do some governments earn trust while others struggle to do so? Why can two countries with similar histories develop in opposite political directions? And why do ideas about power, freedom, justice, and responsibility look different across societies?

Comparative politics gives us a way to study these questions with care. It teaches us to look beyond headlines, to examine how political institutions work, to understand why citizens participate in different ways, and to see the connections between economic change, demographic shifts, and state capacity. Most importantly, it encourages us to compare, not to judge, but to learn.

This book was written to support you as you build these skills. Each essay shows how political concepts become real in the lives of people around the world. The matrices at the back of the book help you see patterns quickly and clearly. As you read, remember that no political system is simple. Every country has strengths and weaknesses, periods of stability and periods of crisis. Your goal as a student is not to memorize facts, but to understand how political structures shape human experience.

If you approach this work with curiosity, empathy, and a willingness to look closely at evidence, you will discover that comparative politics is not only a subject to study—it is a tool for understanding the world you live in.

Welcome to the study of global politics. I hope these pages help you ask better questions, think more clearly, and see more deeply.

— *Harold M. Hutchings*

Author's Note: Teaching Philosophy

Teaching comparative politics is more than guiding students through terms, charts, and case studies. It is helping them understand how people live, how governments make choices, and how power shapes opportunity. My goal as a teacher is to make complex subjects clear and to give students tools they can use long after the course ends.

I believe students learn best when ideas feel connected to real life. When they see how institutions influence everyday decisions or how demographic change affects a nation's future, the subject becomes meaningful. Good teaching makes these connections visible. Strong learning comes from asking questions, testing ideas, and building arguments based on evidence.

I also believe in creating a classroom where every student feels respected. Comparative politics requires empathy and care. We study countries with different histories, cultures, and political traditions. Approaching these topics with humility helps students grow into thoughtful global citizens.

This book reflects these values. The essays aim to explain political systems clearly and fairly. The comparison charts offer structure when the details feel overwhelming. And the entire text is designed to support both students and teachers as they move through a challenging and rewarding subject.

If this book helps you think more deeply, question more confidently, and understand the world more clearly, then it has succeeded in its purpose.

Editorial Preface

This book is built on a simple idea: students learn comparative politics best when they work with clear explanations and trustworthy evidence. To support that goal, every essay and comparison table in this book draws on reliable, publicly available data used by researchers, universities, and international organizations around the world.

The sources fall into three main groups. The first includes global data providers such as the United Nations, the World Bank, and Our World in Data. These organizations collect statistics on population, development, governance, and the environment. Their figures allow us to compare countries using shared measurements rather than assumptions.

The second group consists of widely used political research institutions, including Freedom House, the Varieties of Democracy (V-Dem) Institute, and International IDEA. These organizations specialize in questions of democracy, legitimacy, civil liberties, and electoral systems. Their indicators help students understand how political institutions function and why systems differ in practice.

The third source is the AP Comparative Government Course and Exam Description and the coursebook by Ethel Wood. These texts outline the concepts and case-study structures that guide students through the Big Six countries. They ensure that the essays speak directly to the themes and skills expected in AP classrooms.

All data and descriptions were checked for accuracy and consistency across multiple sources. The aim is not to promote any political view but to help students examine evidence and build arguments. When political conditions change, students should consult updated datasets; the method presented here will help them evaluate new information with confidence.

These essays were written with clarity and accessibility in mind, while still reflecting the complexity of global politics. The goal is to give students a strong foundation for understanding institutions, legitimacy, participation, and political change, and to help teachers guide them through thoughtful, respectful analysis.

Each essay in this volume is paired with comparative tables and matrices in the appendices. These appendices provide a systematic cross-national comparison of regime type, institutional capacity, participation, and policy outcomes across the six AP Comparative Government cases. The essays interpret and explain these patterns rather than reproduce them.

Statement of Academic Integrity

This book is meant to support thoughtful study and honest academic work. Comparative politics requires careful reading, clear writing, and respectful engagement with evidence. Students using this text are expected to express their own ideas, cite their sources, and approach political topics with accuracy and fairness.

The essays and comparison tables in this book are tools for learning, not shortcuts. They offer explanations, examples, and frameworks that can help students develop their own arguments. They should not be copied or presented as original work. Instead, students should use them to deepen understanding and build confidence in reading data, forming claims, and connecting evidence to political concepts.

Academic integrity is a shared responsibility. Teachers guide students in developing strong habits of inquiry, and students commit to completing their work with honesty. When both groups take these commitments seriously, classrooms become places of trust where real learning can happen.

By using this book, you agree to uphold these values and to approach your studies with integrity, respect, and sincerity.

Student Pledge for Respectful Political Learning

Studying comparative politics means learning about countries with different histories, cultures, and belief systems. To understand these differences, students must approach political discussions with care and respect. By using this book, you agree to the following pledge:

I will listen with an open mind.
Different political systems reflect different experiences. I will try to understand ideas before reacting to them.

I will speak respectfully.
I will share my thoughts without attacking others and will challenge ideas, not people.

I will use evidence when making claims.
Strong arguments come from data, sources, and careful reasoning. I will rely on facts rather than stereotypes or assumptions.

I will recognize the dignity of every society we study.
No country is perfect, and no country is without value. I will approach each case study with fairness, empathy, and humility.

I will be responsible with sensitive topics.
Some political issues can feel personal or emotional. I will handle them thoughtfully and respect the experiences of others.

I will uphold academic integrity.
My work will reflect my own thinking, and I will give credit when I use ideas or information from others.

By making this pledge, I commit to helping create a learning environment where everyone feels safe to ask questions, explore ideas, and grow as informed global citizens.

Mission & Values of Mr. Hutchings History

Mr. Hutchings History is built on the belief that every student deserves clear explanations, accessible resources, and a supportive path into complex subjects. Its mission is to help students think critically about the world through high-quality materials that bring global politics and history to life.

The mission is simple:
To make rigorous academic ideas understandable and usable for learners everywhere.

This work is guided by values that shape every lesson and teaching tool:

Clarity. Students should never feel lost in vocabulary or overwhelmed by jargon. Concepts are explained directly to build understanding.

Accuracy. Historical and political information is checked against reliable sources so students and teachers can trust the material.

Respect. Classrooms include people with diverse cultures and beliefs. Materials are culturally sensitive, globally aware, and inclusive.

Integrity. Strong learning depends on honest work. Resources encourage independent thinking and responsible use of evidence.

Accessibility. Resources are written for multilingual learners, using clear language without sacrificing substance.

Curiosity. Learning begins with questions. Students are encouraged to explore ideas and challenge assumptions.

Meet the Author

Harold M. Hutchings is a career educator and teaching historian. He has taught exam board topics for College Board Advanced Placement (AP), International Baccalaureate Diploma Programs (IBDPs), and International General Certificate of Secondary Education (IGCSE), as well as British curriculum A-Levels. His work centers on helping students understand how political systems shape the world around them and how historical ideas connect to current global challenges.

He is the creator of *Mr. Hutchings History*, a teaching brand dedicated to producing clear, accessible, and well-structured resources for diverse classrooms. His materials are used by students and educators seeking both academic rigor and supportive explanations that make complex subjects easier to understand.

Throughout his career, Hutchings has focused on helping learners think critically, write confidently, and approach political topics with respect and empathy. He designs his lessons with multilingual and international students in mind, building bridges between challenging content and real understanding.

This book reflects his commitment to clarity, fairness, and strong academic practice. By blending analytical essays with comparative data and student-friendly explanations, he aims to make comparative politics meaningful for students preparing for the AP exam, and for anyone interested in understanding how governments work in a rapidly changing world.

AI Assistance & Transparency Disclaimer

This book was researched, outlined, and conceptually developed by the author, Harold M. Hutchings. All ideas, interpretations, arguments, and conclusions reflect the author's own academic judgment and teaching experience.

Artificial intelligence tools were used in limited ways to support the writing process. These tools assisted with grammar refinement, formatting consistency, and the organization of material. They also helped strengthen clarity for multilingual and international student audiences. At every stage, the author reviewed, edited, and approved all content to ensure accuracy, alignment with course standards, and the integrity of the final text.

No AI system independently generated research claims, political interpretations, or pedagogical conclusions. All data and analysis come from verified sources, including the United Nations, the World Bank, V-Dem, Freedom House, International IDEA, and the AP Comparative Government Course and Exam Description.

This disclaimer is provided voluntarily to maintain transparency and uphold professional and academic standards in published work.

Contents

Part I

Foundations of Comparative Government

Chapter 1: How to Use This Book

This book is designed to help you understand the major ideas, structures, and patterns that shape political systems around the world. You will find narrative essays, data comparisons, and reference charts that work together to show how governments function and why countries develop in different ways. Each part of the book serves a specific purpose, and knowing how to use it will help you learn more effectively.

The essays form the core of the book. Each one explains a major theme in comparative politics; legitimacy, institutions, civil society, elections, liberalization, political change, demographics, and environmental capacity. These essays show how ideas connect across different countries and why certain political conditions produce similar or different outcomes. They also give you examples you can use in writing, discussion, and exam preparation.

After the essays, the comparison charts offer a clear view of patterns across the six AP case countries: the United Kingdom, China, Russia, Iran, Mexico, and Nigeria. These matrices summarize key information in a format that is easy to study quickly. They help you see relationships, contrasts, and trends at a glance. Many students use these charts to prepare for FRQ 2 and FRQ 3, where comparisons and data interpretation are essential.

Teachers can use the essays for classroom discussion, lesson introductions, or deeper explorations of a topic. The tables can be used as lecture support, handouts, or visual references for exam review. Students can use the essays to build background knowledge and the charts to reinforce understanding or prepare for assessments.

Throughout the book, you will find definitions, clear explanations, and examples that support multilingual and international learners. If something feels unfamiliar, return to the matrices, they often provide the clearest starting point.

This book is meant to be flexible. You can read it straight through or move directly to the sections most helpful for your current unit. The goal is not only to help you succeed in AP Comparative Government, but to strengthen your ability to read political systems thoughtfully and responsibly.

Chapter 2: How to Evaluate Political Sources

Comparative politics relies on evidence. To understand how governments work, students must look at information carefully and judge whether it is reliable, fair, and useful. This chapter introduces a practical approach to evaluating political sources so you can build strong arguments and avoid common mistakes.

When you read a political source, the first question to ask is who created it. Government agencies, international organizations, journalists, independent researchers, and advocacy groups all produce information, but each has different goals. Institutions such as the United Nations, the World Bank, Freedom House, and the Varieties of Democracy (V-Dem) Institute gather data using transparent methods. Their work is widely used in research because they clearly explain how they measure political rights, state capacity, or demographic indicators. When a source is transparent about how it collects information, it becomes easier to trust the results.

The next step is to consider why the source was created. Some reports aim to describe conditions; others seek to persuade. A government might highlight successes and minimize weaknesses. A non-governmental organization may focus on human rights violations to encourage action. A news article may interpret events based on the writer's perspective or the publication's editorial style. Being aware of purpose helps you understand possible biases without rejecting the source entirely.

You should also examine how current the information is. Political conditions change quickly. An election, reform, protest movement, or economic crisis can reshape a country in a short period of time. The best practice is to look for the most recent version of a dataset or report and check whether trends have shifted since it was published.

After asking these questions, focus on how the information is presented. Reliable sources show their methods, define terms clearly, and explain how they reached their conclusions. If a report makes strong claims without explaining how the evidence was gathered, it should be used with caution. Good political analysis uses multiple sources, not just one, to build a complete picture.

Finally, consider how the source fits into your argument. A dataset might show long-term trends. A news article might give context for recent events. A scholarly report might explain why a pattern exists. No source is perfect on its own, but together they help you see how political systems operate.

Evaluating sources is not about finding one that agrees with you. It is about understanding where information comes from, how it was produced, and how it can be used responsibly. When you approach sources with curiosity and discipline, you strengthen your ability to write clearly, argue effectively, and learn with integrity.

Chapter 3: Understanding Comparative Data

Comparative politics depends on shared measurements. When we study six very different countries, we need indicators that allow us to make fair comparisons. This chapter introduces the main data sources used in this book and explains how to read them with confidence.

One of the most common political datasets is produced by Freedom House. Their annual *Freedom in the World* report scores countries on political rights and civil liberties. The scale ranges from 0 to 100, with higher scores showing stronger protections. While no single number can capture all political experiences, the score helps identify broad differences between open democracies, hybrid systems, and authoritarian states. When you see the United Kingdom with a high score and China or Iran with much lower scores, you are seeing a summary of meaningful patterns in political life.

Another important source is the Varieties of Democracy (V-Dem) Institute. V-Dem collects hundreds of indicators, from judicial independence to media freedom. These indicators come from expert surveys and transparent scoring methods. V-Dem helps students understand political nuances that simple categories overlook. For example, Russia and Iran both restrict political competition, but the reasons and mechanisms differ. V-Dem's detailed measures reveal these distinctions.

Many of the demographic indicators in this book come from the United Nations, especially the *World Population Prospects* and *World Urbanization Prospects*. These datasets show trends in fertility, aging, youth populations, and urban growth. They help explain why some governments face mounting pressure, such as pension costs in aging societies or employment needs in countries with large youth populations. Demographic context is essential for understanding long-term political stability.

The World Bank provides two major forms of data used here. The *World Development Indicators (WDI)* offer statistics on economic performance, including GDP, growth rates, and development levels. The *Worldwide Governance Indicators (WGI)* measure government effectiveness, rule of law, corruption control, and regulatory quality. These numbers help students see how well governments implement policies, deliver services, and manage public expectations.

Environmental comparisons often rely on datasets from Our World in Data. These sources show patterns in pollution, emissions, water scarcity, and ecological vulnerability. Environmental stress does not affect all countries equally, and these figures help explain why some governments struggle more than others to maintain stability.

When you read these indicators, remember that each dataset has strengths and limitations. No single measure is perfect, but when used together, they give a fuller picture of how political systems function. The key is not to memorize numbers but to understand what they reveal about capacity, legitimacy, participation, and change.

Learning to read comparative data strengthens your ability to answer FRQs and form evidence-based arguments. It also teaches an important lesson: meaningful political analysis always begins with careful attention to evidence.

Chapter 4: How the Essays Strengthen AP FRQs

The essays in this book were written not only to explain political systems but also to help you build the specific skills needed for the AP Comparative Government and Politics exam. Each essay connects directly to one or more Free-Response Questions (FRQs). When you understand how these connections work, the exam becomes much easier to approach with confidence.

FRQ 1: Concept Application asks you to define political ideas and apply them to real situations. The essays give clear explanations of legitimacy, state capacity, civil society, authoritarian control, electoral rules, economic liberalization, demographic pressure, and environmental stress. As you read, notice how each concept appears in different countries. These examples become the evidence you can use when crafting your responses.

FRQ 2: Quantitative Analysis requires you to interpret charts and data. The matrices in this book show how to compare indicators across the Big Six using real sources such as the United Nations, the World Bank, and Freedom House. The essays also explain what these numbers mean and why certain countries score higher or lower. When you practice reading these tables, you become more comfortable explaining patterns and drawing conclusions based on evidence.

FRQ 3: Comparative Analysis asks you to make direct comparisons between countries. The essays were structured with this skill in mind. They discuss how political institutions differ between systems, how participation varies across regimes, and how demographic and environmental pressures affect stability. When you see phrases like "while Russia… whereas Nigeria…" or "in contrast to the United Kingdom…," you are seeing models of the comparative writing you will use on the exam.

FRQ 4: Argument Essay requires you to make a claim and support it with evidence from the Big Six. The essays offer ready-made examples of how an argument develops from a clear idea to a supported explanation. They show how to link concepts like legitimacy, institutions, or liberalization to specific outcomes in different political systems. The goal is not to memorize the essays but to see how good arguments are built, and then create your own.

When you use this book, think of each essay as a guide to both understanding content and strengthening your writing. As you read, ask yourself: *What concept is being explained? How is it applied to a country? How could I use this example in an FRQ?* If you read with these questions in mind, you will gain both knowledge and confidence.

These essays are tools. They help you understand political ideas, interpret data, compare systems, and build arguments. With practice, you will find that the skills you develop here extend beyond the exam and help you read global events with maturity and insight.

Part II

Analytical Essays

Essay 1

What Makes Power Legitimate? A Cross-Country Analysis of Authority and Trust

Political power endures not simply because it is exercised, but because it is accepted. Governments rule most effectively when citizens believe that authority is rightful, justified, and meaningful. This belief, commonly described as political legitimacy, forms the foundation of political stability. Where legitimacy is strong, states govern through consent and predictable institutions. Where it is weak, rulers must rely more heavily on coercion, nationalism, ideology, or economic performance to maintain control. Comparative politics, therefore, treats legitimacy not as a moral label but as a functional relationship between authority and belief, one that varies sharply across regime types and historical contexts.

The United Kingdom represents a case in which legitimacy is deeply institutionalized. Its parliamentary system, constitutional conventions, and long-standing rule of law have produced stable expectations about how power is exercised and transferred, as summarized in Appendix C.[1] Citizens generally accept electoral outcomes, judicial decisions, and executive authority even when they strongly oppose particular policies. This acceptance is rooted less in ideology than in trust that institutions operate fairly and predictably. Comparative data consistently show high levels of political rights and civil liberties in the British system, a pattern reflected in both country assessments and cross-national ratings.[2] Even periods of acute political tension, such as the Brexit process, did not undermine the core legitimacy of the state. Instead,

---

[1] Appendix C, Figure C1, "Parliamentary System (United Kingdom)"
[2] Freedom House, *Freedom in the World 2023: Marking 50 Years in the Struggle for Democracy* (Washington, DC: Freedom House, 2023), 1279–1285, 1487–1489

conflict was channeled through elections, parliamentary debate, and judicial review, reinforcing rather than weakening institutional authority. Comparative legitimacy patterns show that the United Kingdom derives authority primarily from institutional continuity, procedural fairness, and the rule of law rather than from economic performance or charismatic leadership. This pattern is summarized in Appendix A, which contrasts Britain's institutional foundations with performance-based and ideological legitimacy in other systems.

China illustrates a fundamentally different pathway to legitimacy. The Chinese Communist Party does not rely on competitive elections to justify its rule. Instead, it emphasizes performance, national unity, and historical narratives of stability after chaos. Since the late twentieth century, rapid economic growth, poverty reduction, and infrastructure expansion have reinforced public acceptance of centralized authority. World Bank governance indicators consistently rate China highly in government effectiveness, reflecting strong administrative capacity and coordinated policy implementation, even as political participation remains tightly constrained.[3] Comparative scholarship on regime durability suggests that public support plays a critical role in sustaining political systems. Claassen shows that legitimacy rooted in citizen attitudes strengthens regime endurance, particularly where institutional arrangements already exist, while other research highlights how authoritarian systems rely on performance-based legitimacy and nationalist narratives when electoral accountability is absent. In such systems, legitimacy is conditional rather than procedural, as citizens tolerate limited

---

[3] World Bank, *Worldwide Governance Indicators:* "Government Effectiveness" (Washington, DC: World Bank Group, 2023); Freedom House, *Freedom in the World 2023*, 269–276

political choice in exchange for order, development, and state competence.[4]

Russia demonstrates how legitimacy weakens when institutions appear hollow. While elections are held regularly, political competition is tightly managed, independent media are restricted, and opposition actors are marginalized. The state frames centralized authority as necessary for stability, sovereignty, and national strength, particularly in the face of perceived external threats. Yet Freedom House consistently records low scores for political rights and civil liberties, reflecting constrained participation and weak institutional accountability.[5] Governance indicators also reveal uneven service delivery and persistent corruption, particularly outside major urban centers.[6] Comparative studies of hybrid regimes show that legitimacy in such systems depends heavily on nationalism, symbolic elections, and control of information rather than genuine belief in institutional fairness. When economic performance falters or repression intensifies, legitimacy becomes increasingly fragile, sustained more by coercion than consent. These contrasting sources of legitimacy—procedural in the United Kingdom, performance-based in China, and ideological or nationalist in Iran and Russia—help explain why citizen trust, participation, and regime stability take such different forms across cases, a pattern made visible when legitimacy is viewed comparatively rather than country by country.[7]

---

[4] Christopher Claassen, *Does Public Support Help Democracy Survive?* (unpublished manuscript, 2019), 1–2, 26–27; Andrea Kendall-Taylor, Erica Frantz, and Joseph Wright, "The Digital Dictators: How Technology Strengthens Autocracy," *Foreign Affairs* (2020)

[5] Freedom House, *Freedom in the World 2023*, 1109–1116, 1487–1489

[6] World Bank, *Worldwide Governance Indicators*, "Government Effectiveness; Control of Corruption"

[7] See Appendix A, Table A3, "Political Participation and Civil Society Constraints"

Iran presents a distinct hybrid form of legitimacy rooted in ideology and religious authority. Its political system combines republican institutions such as elections and a legislature with clerical oversight under the doctrine of *Velayat-e Faqih*. For some citizens, particularly older or more conservative constituencies, religious leadership provides moral legitimacy and protection against foreign influence. At the same time, repeated protest movements and declining electoral participation reveal growing disillusionment, especially among younger citizens. Demographic pressures intensify this tension: a majority of Iran's population is under thirty-five,[8] creating a large youth cohort whose political and economic expectations increasingly strain existing institutions.[9] Scholarly research on protest and electoral activism in Iran suggests that controlled elections can mobilize participation while simultaneously exposing regime constraints, producing cycles of engagement, repression, and declining trust rather than durable legitimacy.[10]

Mexico illustrates the volatility of legitimacy during democratic consolidation. After decades of one-party dominance, electoral reforms and institutional restructuring produced competitive elections and peaceful alternation of power. Independent electoral authorities strengthened procedural credibility, and formal democratic rules gained broad acceptance. Yet legitimacy remains uneven. Corruption, organized crime, and weak rule of law undermine confidence in government authority,

---

[8] As summarized in Appendix B, Table B1, "Economic Liberalization and State Capacity"; See Appendix B, *Comparative Indicators and Structural Pressures,* for comparative indicators

[9] United Nations, Department of Economic and Social Affairs, Population Division, *World Population Prospects 2022: Summary of Results* (New York: United Nations, 2022), 22

[10] Mohammad Ali Kadivar and Vahid Abedini, "Electoral Activism in Iran: A Mechanism for Political Change," *Comparative Politics* 52, no. 3 (2020), 1–3, 16–17

particularly at the local level. Mexico's mid-range Freedom House ratings and moderate government effectiveness scores reflect this mixed reality: democratic institutions exist and function, but capacity constraints and security failures limit their ability to generate sustained public confidence in government institutions.[11] Comparative research on democratic satisfaction indicates that legitimacy depends not only on electoral procedures but also on the state's ability to provide security and basic services, a challenge Mexico continues to face.

Nigeria confronts the most acute legitimacy challenges among the six cases examined. It is a federal democracy with regular elections, high voter engagement, and a vibrant civil society. Yet chronic insecurity, corruption, and uneven state presence weaken trust in institutions. Nigeria ranks among the lowest globally on government effectiveness indicators,[12] reflecting limited administrative reach and uneven service provision across regions.[13] Demographic pressures further complicate legitimacy. Nigeria's large and youthful population places sustained demographic pressure on state,[14] intensifying governance challenges in a context of limited administrative reach.[15] Comparative studies of fragile democracies note that high participation without corresponding improvements in governance can intensify frustration, producing a paradox of high civic engagement alongside persistently low institutional trust.[16]

---

[11] Freedom House, *Freedom in the World 2023*, 1021–1028, 1487–1489; World Bank, *Worldwide Governance Indicators*

[12] As summarized in Appendix B, Table B2, "Demographic Pressures and Population Structure"

[13] World Bank, *Worldwide Governance Indicators*, "Government Effectiveness"

[14] As summarized in Appendix B, Table B1

[15] United Nations, *World Population Prospects 2022*, 23

[16] Jeremiah O. Arowosegbe, "Nigeria at Sixty: A Failure That Succeeded," *Journal of the Historical Society of Nigeria* 29 (2020): 2–3, 6–7, 18–20, JSTOR.

Taken together, these six cases demonstrate that legitimacy is neither singular nor static. In the United Kingdom, legitimacy flows primarily from institutional stability and procedural trust. In China, it is grounded in performance and administrative capacity. In Russia and Iran, legitimacy depends heavily on nationalism, ideology, and controlled participation. In Mexico and Nigeria, legitimacy is continually renegotiated as democratic institutions operate under conditions of limited capacity and social strain. Across all cases, legitimacy shapes how power is exercised, how citizens respond to authority, and how resilient political systems prove under stress. The cross-national patterns discussed in this essay become clearest when viewed comparatively, where each country's source of authority can be seen operating within distinct regimes of accountability and control.[17]

Understanding legitimacy is, therefore, central to comparative government. It explains why some regimes endure despite limited freedom, why others struggle despite formal democracy, and why political stability cannot be measured by institutions alone. Legitimacy determines whether power is experienced as rightful or imposed, and whether political order rests on consent or compulsion. For students and teachers of comparative politics, legitimacy is not merely a concept to define, but a lens through which political success, failure, and change can be systematically understood.

---

[17] Appendix A

Further Reading for Teachers

The following scholarly sources support and extend the arguments in this essay. They are well-suited for teacher enrichment, lesson design, or advanced student reading.

Arowosegbe, Jeremiah O. "Nigeria at Sixty: A Failure That Succeeded." *Journal of the Historical Society of Nigeria* 29 (2020): 1–20.
Provides historical context for Nigeria's legitimacy challenges and federal governance tensions.
Claassen, Christopher. "Does Public Support Help Democracy Survive?" *American Journal of Political Science* 64, no. 1 (2020): 118–134.
Explores the relationship between public trust and regime stability across democratic and non-democratic systems.
Claassen, Christopher, and Pedro C. Magalhães. "Do the Rich and the Poor Have Different Conceptions of Democracy?" *Comparative Politics* 52, no. 2 (2020): 241–65.
Useful for understanding legitimacy gaps in unequal democracies such as Mexico and Nigeria.
Kadivar, Mohammad Ali, and Vahid Abedini. "Electoral Activism in Iran." *Comparative Politics* 52, no. 3 (2020): 395–418.
Examines how participation in constrained electoral systems can both sustain and undermine legitimacy.
Kendall-Taylor, Andrea, Erica Frantz, and Joseph Wright. "The Digital Dictators." *Foreign Affairs* 99, no. 2 (2020): 103–15.
Analyzes how modern authoritarian regimes, including Russia and China, reinforce legitimacy through technology and information control.

Essay 1 Bibliography

Arowosegbe, Jeremiah O. "Nigeria at Sixty: A Failure That Succeeded." *Journal of the Historical Society of Nigeria* 29 (2020): 1–20.

Claassen, Christopher. *Does Public Support Help Democracy Survive?* Manuscript, 2019, https://www.chrisclaassen.com/docs/Claassen_democracy_public_support.pdf

Freedom House. *Freedom in the World 2023: Marking 50 Years in the Struggle for Democracy.* Washington, DC: Freedom House, 2023.

Kadivar, Mohammad Ali, and Vahid Abedini. "Electoral Activism in Iran." *Comparative Politics* 52, no. 3 (2020): 395–418.

Kendall-Taylor, Andrea, Erica Frantz, and Joseph Wright. "The Digital Dictators: How Technology Strengthens Autocracy." *Foreign Affairs*, February 6, 2020. Author PDF, Internet Archive. https://archive.org/details/The-Digital-Dictators-How-Technology-Strengthens-Autocracy

United Nations, Department of Economic and Social Affairs, Population Division. *World Population Prospects 2022: Summary of Results.* New York: United Nations, 2022. https://www.un.org/development/desa/pd/content/World-Population-Prospects-2022.

World Bank. *Worldwide Governance Indicators.* Washington, DC: World Bank Group, 2023. https://www.worldbank.org/en/publication/worldwide-governance-indicators.

Why Do Political Institutions Matter? How Structures Shape Policy, Participation, and Stability

Political institutions shape how power is organized, exercised, and constrained. They determine who governs, how leaders are selected, how policy is made, and how citizens participate in political life. While history, culture, and economic conditions influence political outcomes, institutions provide the framework within which these forces operate. As a result, similar social or economic challenges often produce different political responses because institutions channel conflict, cooperation, and accountability in distinct ways. Institutions do not act independently of society, but their structure strongly influences whether political systems generate stability, responsiveness, or crisis.

Parliamentary systems illustrate how institutional design can promote coordination and continuity. In the United Kingdom, the executive emerges from the legislature and remains dependent on parliamentary confidence.[1] This fusion of powers encourages negotiation within parties and reduces the likelihood of prolonged conflict between branches. Policy change is often smoother because the executive and legislative majority typically act in concert. Leadership transitions occur through established procedures such as votes of no confidence or party leadership contests, reinforcing predictability and legitimacy. Parliamentary oversight mechanisms, a professional and politically neutral civil service, and an independent judiciary operating under the rule of law contribute to institutional stability by constraining executive

---

[1] As can be seen in Appendix C, Figure C1, "Parliamentary System (United Kingdom)"

power and ensuring continuity of governance.[2] The British case shows that institutional resilience stems less from rigid design than from clearly defined rules of accountability and authority, a pattern that becomes especially clear when compared across systems.[3]

Presidential systems organize power differently by separating the election and authority of the executive and legislature. This structure allows voters to hold each branch accountable independently, but it also increases the potential for institutional conflict. Mexico's experience demonstrates both the promise and limits of this model. Electoral reforms in the late twentieth century strengthened independent electoral institutions and expanded congressional authority, ending decades of one-party dominance. These changes improved political competition and representation, yet institutional performance remains uneven. Corruption, organized crime, and weak rule of law continue to constrain policy effectiveness, limiting the ability of democratic institutions to generate sustained public confidence in government institutions.[4] Institutions exist and function, but their capacity to deliver consistent governance remains contested. These institutional contrasts, parliamentary fusion of powers, presidential separation, and hybrid concentration, are outlined systematically in the institutional structure tables.[5]

Nigeria's presidential system faces even greater strain. Although its constitution distributes power across a federal structure, weak coordination between national and state

---

[2] Ethel Wood, *AP Comparative Government & Politics: An Essential Coursebook* (New York: WoodYard Publications, 2013), 97–101, 108–114

[3] As shown in Appendix A, Table A2, "Institutional Configuration and Distribution of Political Power"

[4] Freedom House, *Freedom in the World 2023: Marking 50 Years in the Struggle for Democracy* (Washington, DC: Freedom House, 2023), 1021–1028, 1487–1489; World Bank, *Worldwide Governance Indicators*

[5] See Appendix A, *Comparative Political and Institutional Frameworks.*

governments undermines institutional effectiveness.[6] Insecurity, corruption, and uneven administrative capacity weaken the state's ability to enforce policy or provide services. Nigeria ranks low on government effectiveness indicators,[7] reflecting limited bureaucratic reach and uneven governance across regions.[8] Scholarly analyses of Nigerian federalism note that institutional fragmentation, combined with demographic pressure and regional inequality, limits the capacity of formal structures to translate political participation into stability or policy coherence.[9] The result is a system in which democratic procedures coexist with persistent institutional weakness.

Semi-presidential systems combine elements of parliamentary and presidential design, but outcomes depend heavily on political context. Russia formally divides executive authority between a president and a prime minister; however, over time, power has become increasingly centralized in the presidency. Constitutional authority, control over security services, and dominance of political parties have reduced legislative independence and judicial autonomy. While this concentration of power enhances the state's ability to act decisively, it also limits accountability and constrains political competition. Freedom House documents extensive restrictions on opposition activity and media freedom, illustrating how institutional design can be reshaped in practice to reinforce executive dominance.[10] Comparative research on hybrid regimes suggests that such systems often retain the appearance of institutional balance while hollowing out its substance.

---

[6] See Appendix C, Figure C2, "Presidential System (Mexico, Nigeria)"
[7] See Appendix B, Table B2, "Demographic Pressures and Population Structure"
[8] World Bank, *Worldwide Governance Indicators*: "Government Effectiveness"
[9] Jeremiah O. Arowosegbe, "Nigeria at Sixty: A Failure That Succeeded," *Journal of the Historical Society of Nigeria* 29 (2020): 3–5, 9–11, 18–20, JSTOR.
[10] Freedom House, *Freedom in the World 2023*, 1109–1116

Iran demonstrates how institutions can blend electoral mechanisms with ideological oversight. Citizens elect a president and a legislature, yet unelected bodies, such as the Supreme Leader and the Guardian Council, retain authority to vet candidates and review legislation.[11] This structure creates recurring tension between elected officials seeking reform and clerical institutions enforcing ideological boundaries. Participation is permitted, but tightly constrained. Comparative studies of Iran's electoral politics show that these institutional arrangements can mobilize voters while simultaneously limiting policy change, producing cycles of engagement, frustration, and protest rather than sustained policy responsiveness.[12] Institutions thus shape not only who participates, but how far participation can translate into change.

China presents the most centralized institutional model among the cases examined. The Chinese Communist Party controls the executive, legislature, and judiciary, eliminating formal separation of powers. Leadership selection occurs through internal party processes rather than competitive elections, enabling long-term planning and coordinated policy implementation. China ranks high on the World Bank's Government Effectiveness indicator, reflecting strong administrative capacity and bureaucratic discipline.[13] However, accountability flows upward within the party rather than outward to the public. Institutions are stable and effective in policy execution, but closed to independent participation. Comparative scholarship emphasizes that such

---

[11] As seen in Appendix C, Figure C5, "Iran's Theocratic-Republic Hybrid."

[12] Mohammad Ali Kadivar and Vahid Abedini, "Electoral Activism in Iran: A Mechanism for Political Change," *Comparative Politics* 52, no. 3 (2020), 1–3, 8–10, 15–17

[13] World Bank, *Worldwide Governance Indicators:* "Government Effectiveness" (Washington, DC: World Bank Group, 2023)

systems rely on performance and nationalist legitimacy rather than institutional pluralism to sustain authority.[14]

Federalism further illustrates how similar institutional designs can yield different outcomes. The United Kingdom remains formally unitary, yet devolution has transferred meaningful authority to Scotland, Wales, and Northern Ireland. This arrangement accommodates regional diversity while preserving national unity, demonstrating how flexible institutional adaptation can enhance stability. Mexico and Nigeria are constitutionally federal, but their experiences diverge. Mexico's federalism supports political pluralism and regional governance, while Nigeria's federal structure struggles under corruption, weak coordination, and uneven state capacity. Institutional design alone does not determine outcomes; capacity and enforcement shape whether federalism strengthens or fragments the state.

Judicial institutions play a critical role in shaping how political power is constrained. In systems with meaningful judicial independence, courts can protect rights, resolve disputes, and check executive authority. The United Kingdom and Mexico allow judicial review and maintain some degree of insulation from political pressure, though effectiveness varies. In Russia, Iran, and China, judicial institutions exist but are subject to political or ideological influence, limiting their ability to function as independent arbiters. Comparative institutional analyses consistently show that when courts lack autonomy, legal systems reinforce executive power rather than constrain it, weakening accountability and public trust. Taken together, the cases show that institutional design shapes political outcomes by structuring how power is exercised and constrained, a relationship that

---

[14] Andrea Kendall-Taylor, Erica Frantz, and Joseph Wright, "The Digital Dictators: How Technology Strengthens Autocracy," *Foreign Affairs* (2020)

becomes clearer when regime type and state capacity are considered side by side.[15]

Across these cases, institutions matter not only because of how they are designed, but because of how they operate in practice. They shape participation, channel conflict, and influence whether power is exercised transparently or concentrated behind closed doors. Strong institutions foster accountability, predictability, and trust. Weak, constrained, or manipulated institutions limit meaningful participation and concentrate authority, often producing long-term challenges for stability and legitimacy. Political institutions do not eliminate conflict or inequality, but they structure how societies confront them. For students of comparative government, institutions are therefore central not because they explain everything, but because they shape the conditions under which everything else occurs.

---

[15] Appendix A

Further Reading for Teachers

The following scholarly sources deepen understanding of institutional design, regime types, and political accountability across the AP Comparative Government cases.

Arowosegbe, Jeremiah O. "Nigeria at Sixty: A Failure That Succeeded." *Journal of the Historical Society of Nigeria* 29 (2020): 1–20.
  Provides historical and institutional context for Nigeria's federal and presidential challenges.

Claassen, Christopher. "Does Public Support Help Democracy Survive?" *American Journal of Political Science* 64, no. 1 (2020): 118–134.
  Useful for linking institutional performance to public trust and regime durability.

Kadivar, Mohammad Ali, and Vahid Abedini. "Electoral Activism in Iran." *Comparative Politics* 52, no. 3 (2020): 395–418.
  Explores participation and constraint within hybrid electoral-religious institutions.

Kendall-Taylor, Andrea, Erica Frantz, and Joseph Wright. "The Digital Dictators." *Foreign Affairs* 99, no. 2 (2020): 103–15.
  Examines how authoritarian institutions adapt to maintain control and policy capacity.

Zagrebina, Anna. "Concepts of Democracy in Democratic and Nondemocratic Countries." *International Political Science Review* 41, no. 4 (2020): 482–498.
  Helpful for classroom discussion on how institutional contexts shape political expectations.

Essay 2 Bibliography

Arowosegbe, Jeremiah O. "Nigeria at Sixty: A Failure That Succeeded." *Journal of the Historical Society of Nigeria* 29 (2020): 1–20.

Freedom House. *Freedom in the World 2023: Marking 50 Years in the Struggle for Democracy.* Washington, DC: Freedom House, 2023.

Kadivar, Mohammad Ali, and Vahid Abedini. "Electoral Activism in Iran." *Comparative Politics* 52, no. 3 (2020): 395–418.

Kendall-Taylor, Andrea, Erica Frantz, and Joseph Wright. "The Digital Dictators: How Technology Strengthens Autocracy." *Foreign Affairs*, vol. 99, no. 2, 2020, pp. 103–115.

Wood, Ethel. *AP Comparative Government & Politics: An Essential Coursebook.* 6th ed. New York: WoodYard Publications, 2013.

World Bank. *Worldwide Governance Indicators.* Washington, DC: World Bank Group, 2023. https://www.worldbank.org/en/publication/worldwide-governance-indicators.

The Role of Civil Society in Democratization and Authoritarian Control

Civil society refers to the sphere of organized social life that exists outside the formal structures of the state. It includes labor unions, professional associations, student movements, religious organizations, advocacy groups, independent media, and increasingly, digital networks. Civil society matters because it creates channels for participation that do not rely on government authority. Through these channels, citizens can express interests, share information, and mobilize collectively. The strength, independence, and boundaries of civil society therefore reveal much about how power operates within a political system. Where civil society is open and protected, political participation expands and accountability deepens. Where it is constrained or co-opted, the state faces fewer challenges and political change becomes more difficult.

In established democracies such as the United Kingdom, civil society plays a central role in public debate and political accountability. Independent media organizations investigate government actions, advocacy groups influence legislative agendas, and voluntary associations mobilize citizens around social and economic concerns. These activities operate within a legal framework that protects freedom of association and expression. Freedom House consistently rates the United Kingdom highly in civil liberties, reflecting the relative openness of its civic space.[1] As a result, civil society acts as a bridge between citizens and institutions, reinforcing democratic legitimacy by offering nonviolent, institutionalized avenues for participation.

---

[1] Freedom House, *Freedom in the World 2023: Marking 50 Years in the Struggle for Democracy* (Washington, DC: Freedom House, 2023), 1279–1285

Comparative research on democratic survival shows that legitimacy rooted in citizen support strengthens democratic stability in such contexts, helping established democracies channel participation without destabilizing the state.[2]

Mexico's experience illustrates how civil society can expand during democratic transition. For much of the twentieth century, political life was dominated by a single party, limiting the influence of independent civic organizations. As electoral reforms increased competition and transparency, journalists, student movements, election-monitoring groups, and advocacy organizations gained greater visibility and influence. These actors pressured institutions to adopt fairer electoral practices and exposed corruption, contributing to democratic consolidation. However, civil society in Mexico continues to operate under significant strain. Violence against journalists, organized crime, and corruption create risks that limit the effectiveness of civic engagement. Despite these constraints, civic organizations remain active in areas such as human rights, indigenous autonomy, gender equality, and anti-corruption efforts, demonstrating that civil society can persist even when institutional protection is uneven.[3] Across the six cases, variation in civil society autonomy reflects how far states are willing to tolerate independent organization, a contrast that reveals the boundary between participation and control in different regimes.[4]

Nigeria highlights both the potential and the limits of civil society in a developing democracy. Civic activism is widespread, encompassing labor unions, professional groups, community associations, and youth-led movements. The #EndSARS protests,

---

[2] Christopher Claassen, *Does Public Support Help Democracy Survive?* (unpublished manuscript, 2019), 1–2, 26–27

[3] Freedom House, *Freedom in the World 2023*, 1021–1028

[4] See Appendix A, Table A3, "Political Participation and Civil Society Constraints"; See Appendix C, Figure C7, "Regime Type Classification Diagram"

driven largely by young Nigerians, drew national and international attention to police brutality and demands for accountability. These mobilizations reflect a vibrant civic culture and a strong willingness to challenge authority. Yet civil society operates in an environment marked by insecurity, economic inequality, and weak state capacity. Nigeria's low ranking on government effectiveness indicators highlights the difficulty of converting civic pressure into consistent policy reform.[5] Scholarly analyses of Nigerian politics emphasize that while civil society can raise awareness and mobilize participation, its impact is often constrained by corruption and limited institutional responsiveness.[6]

In hybrid regimes such as Iran, civil society exists but within tightly controlled boundaries. Professional associations, religious charities, and community organizations operate legally, yet activities perceived as politically threatening face surveillance, censorship, or legal restriction. Students and young people frequently form the backbone of reform-oriented movements, reflecting both demographic pressure and frustration with limited political choice. These movements tend to emerge in cycles, responding to economic hardship, social restrictions, or political exclusion. Comparative studies of Iran's civic activism show that civil society can generate sustained pressure for reform without possessing the institutional leverage necessary to produce fundamental systemic change, particularly when unelected bodies retain veto power over elected institutions.[7]

---

[5] World Bank, *Worldwide Governance Indicators:* "Government Effectiveness" (Washington, DC: World Bank Group, 2023); See Appendix B, Table B2, "Demographic Pressures and Population Structure"

[6] Jeremiah O. Arowosegbe, "Nigeria at Sixty: A Failure That Succeeded," *Journal of the Historical Society of Nigeria* 29 (2020): 6–8, 14–16, 18–20, JSTOR.

[7] Mohammad Ali Kadivar and Vahid Abedini, "Electoral Activism in Iran: A Mechanism for Political Change," *Comparative Politics* 52, no. 3 (2020), 3–5, 9–11, 15–17

Russia demonstrates how authoritarian governments can actively suppress or manage civil society to maintain political control. Independent media outlets, opposition groups, and nongovernmental organizations face restrictive laws, registration requirements, and the designation of "foreign agents." These measures increase legal and financial risk for civic actors and discourage participation. Freedom House records low levels of associational and expressive freedom in Russia, reflecting the systematic narrowing of civic space.[8] Comparative research on authoritarian governance suggests that weakening civil society reduces the flow of alternative information and limits collective action, allowing the state to monopolize political narratives and decision-making.[9]

China presents a distinct model of managed civil society. Local charities, environmental organizations, and professional associations often operate with state approval and may play meaningful roles in service provision or community development. However, organizations that challenge party authority or advocate for political rights face swift restriction. Digital platforms provide spaces for limited expression, yet censorship and surveillance constrain sensitive discussion. This arrangement produces a form of civil society that is active but subordinate. Comparative scholars note that such systems allow civic engagement in nonpolitical domains while preventing the emergence of independent networks capable of challenging regime authority.[10] Civil society thus contributes to governance efficiency without undermining political control.

---

[8] Freedom House, *Freedom in the World 2023*, 1109–1116
[9] Andrea Kendall-Taylor, Erica Frantz, and Joseph Wright, "The Digital Dictators: How Technology Strengthens Autocracy," *Foreign Affairs* (2020)
[10] Zheng Zhu, "Popular Perceptions of Democracy in China," *American Journal of Chinese Studies* 27, no. 2 (2020): 560–563, 570–573

Across these cases, civil society functions differently depending on regime type and institutional openness. In democracies, it expands participation, shapes public debate, and reinforces legitimacy by providing peaceful mechanisms for influence. In hybrid systems, it operates as a pressure valve, expressing demands for reform while remaining constrained by unelected power centers. In authoritarian systems, civil society is permitted only within boundaries that preserve state dominance, and organizations that grow too influential face restriction. The presence, strength, and autonomy of civil society therefore offer critical insight into how governments relate to their citizens. Civil society's varying capacity to pressure the state across regime types is summarized in the appendices, where participation is mapped against accountability and repression.[11]

Civil society does not determine political outcomes on its own, but it shapes the environment in which participation occurs. Where civic organizations can mobilize citizens and circulate information freely, governments face stronger incentives to respond to public concerns. Where civil society is weak or constrained, accountability diminishes, and political systems risk becoming disconnected from society. For students of comparative government, civil society is one of the clearest indicators of whether a political system welcomes engagement or fears it, and whether power is exercised through consent or control.

---

[11] See Appendix A, *Comparative Political and Institutional Frameworks.*

Further Reading for Teachers

The following scholarly sources deepen understanding of civil society's role across democratic and authoritarian contexts and are well-suited for teacher enrichment or advanced classroom use.

Arowosegbe, Jeremiah O. "Nigeria at Sixty: A Failure That Succeeded." *Journal of the Historical Society of Nigeria* 29 (2020): 1–20.
  Provides historical and civic context for Nigeria's activism and governance challenges.
Claassen, Christopher. "Does Public Support Help Democracy Survive?" *American Journal of Political Science* 64, no. 1 (2020): 118–134.
  Connects civic trust and participation to regime stability.
Kadivar, Mohammad Ali, and Vahid Abedini. "Electoral Activism in Iran." *Comparative Politics* 52, no. 3 (2020): 395–418.
  Examines how civil society operates within constrained hybrid systems.
Kendall-Taylor, Andrea, Erica Frantz, and Joseph Wright. "The Digital Dictators." *Foreign Affairs* 99, no. 2 (2020): 103–15.
  Analyzes how authoritarian regimes restrict and reshape civic space.
Zhu, Zheng. "Popular Perceptions of Democracy in China." *American Journal of Chinese Studies* 27, no. 2 (2020): 151–173.
  Useful for understanding state-managed civil society and public expectations.

Essay 3 Bibliography

Arowosegbe, Jeremiah O. "Nigeria at Sixty: A Failure That Succeeded." *Journal of the Historical Society of Nigeria* 29 (2020): 1–20.

Claassen, Christopher. *Does Public Support Help Democracy Survive?* Manuscript, 2019, https://www.chrisclaassen.com/docs/Claassen_democracy_public_support.pdf

Freedom House. *Freedom in the World 2023: Marking 50 Years in the Struggle for Democracy.* Washington, DC: Freedom House, 2023.

Kadivar, Mohammad Ali, and Vahid Abedini. "Electoral Activism in Iran." *Comparative Politics* 52, no. 3 (2020): 395–418.

Kendall-Taylor, Andrea, Erica Frantz, and Joseph Wright. "The Digital Dictators: How Technology Strengthens Autocracy." *Foreign Affairs*, February 6, 2020. Author PDF, Internet Archive. https://archive.org/details/The-Digital-Dictators-How-Technology-Strengthens-Autocracy

World Bank. *Worldwide Governance Indicators.* Washington, DC: World Bank Group, 2023. https://www.worldbank.org/en/publication/worldwide-governance-indicators.

Zhu, Zheng. "Popular Perceptions of Democracy in China." *American Journal of Chinese Studies* 27, no. 2 (2020): 151–173.

Elections and Representation: Who Really Has a Voice?

Elections are commonly treated as the core expression of political participation, yet the presence of voting alone does not guarantee representation. Electoral systems translate votes into power through specific rules that shape competition, determine which voices are amplified, and influence whether citizens believe their participation matters. As a result, elections can function as mechanisms of accountability, instruments of controlled participation, or symbols of legitimacy without meaningful choice. Understanding who truly has a political voice requires examining how electoral rules operate in practice rather than assuming that elections automatically reflect public will.

The United Kingdom illustrates how majoritarian electoral systems shape representation in established democracies. Members of Parliament are elected in single-member districts using first-past-the-post rules, in which the candidate with the most votes wins the seat regardless of overall vote share. This system encourages two dominant parties, simplifies voter choice, and often produces decisive parliamentary majorities capable of governing effectively. Stable cabinets and clear responsibility enhance policy coherence and accountability. However, the same system can distort representation by underrepresenting smaller parties and exaggerating the dominance of large ones. Parties with substantial national support may win few seats, while governments can form without winning a majority of votes. Despite these limitations, elections remain genuinely competitive, and the electoral process retains strong procedural legitimacy even when outcomes are disproportional due to the voting system.[1] The representational trade-offs created by winner-take-all electoral rules trade proportional representation for decisiveness in government formation, a pattern that helps explain both the stability and the representational limits of such systems across cases. [2]

Mexico demonstrates how mixed electoral systems attempt to balance representation and governability. The Chamber of Deputies combines single-member district elections with proportional representation lists, allowing smaller parties to gain seats while preserving district-level accountability.[3] Electoral reforms in the late twentieth century strengthened the independence of election administration and reduced executive interference, ending decades of one-party dominance. These institutional changes expanded political pluralism and improved public confidence in elections. Yet representation remains uneven. Corruption, violence, and intimidation, particularly at the local level, continue to shape voter participation and candidate competition. Comparative assessments show that while mixed systems can broaden representation, their capacity to generate durable legitimacy depends heavily on enforcement and security conditions, as weak implementation undermines public confidence in democratic institutions.[4]

Nigeria's electoral system blends presidential elections with legislative representation through single-member districts. Elections are competitive, and political participation is high,

---

[1] Ethel Wood, *AP Comparative Government & Politics: An Essential Coursebook* (New York: WoodYard Publications, 2013), 103–107

[2] See Appendix A, Table A4, "Electoral Competition and Representation"

[3] See Appendix C, Figure C6, "Electoral Systems Diagram"

[4] Freedom House, *Freedom in the World 2023: Marking 50 Years in the Struggle for Democracy* (Washington, DC: Freedom House, 2023), 1021–1028, 1487–1489; Christopher Claassen, *Does Public Support Help Democracy Survive?* (unpublished manuscript, 2019), 1–2, 26–27

particularly during national contests. However, insecurity, logistical challenges, and allegations of fraud undermine confidence in electoral outcomes. Regional inequality and ethnic divisions further complicate representation, as voters often perceive elections as zero-sum struggles for access to state resources. While the independent electoral commission has made procedural improvements, limited state capacity and uneven enforcement weaken the link between votes and policy outcomes. Scholarly research on electoral participation in fragile democracies highlights that high turnout does not necessarily translate into effective representation when institutional trust and state capacity remain weak.[5]

Russia provides a clear example of elections functioning without meaningful competition. The country employs a mixed electoral system, yet legal rules, media control, and candidate restrictions systematically favor the ruling party. Opposition figures face legal disqualification, limited access to media, and harassment, while civil society organizations monitoring elections operate under pressure. Freedom House records extremely low scores for political rights and civil liberties, noting that elections do not provide voters with a genuine opportunity to alter leadership or policy direction.[6] In this context, elections serve primarily as instruments of regime legitimation rather than channels of representation. Outcomes are shaped by institutional control long before ballots are cast.

Iran offers another model of restricted electoral competition. Citizens vote for a president and parliament, but the Guardian Council vets candidates and disqualifies those deemed unacceptable. This process narrows political choice and prevents reform-oriented candidates from competing fully. Despite these

[5] Jeremiah O. Arowosegbe, "Nigeria at Sixty: A Failure That Succeeded," *Journal of the Historical Society of Nigeria* 29 (2020): 4–6, 11–13, 18–20, JSTOR.
[6] Freedom House, *Freedom in the World 2023*, 1335–1342, 1487–1489

constraints, elections generate significant public engagement, particularly among younger voters who view participation as one of the few available avenues for expression. Comparative research on Iran's electoral politics shows that restricted elections can mobilize voters while simultaneously producing frustration when participation fails to yield meaningful policy change, resulting in recurring cycles of high expectations, institutional blockage, and protest.[7] Across cases, elections range from genuinely competitive to tightly restricted or largely symbolic, a distinction that helps explain why participation translates into influence in some systems but not in others.[8]

China differs fundamentally from the other cases because it does not hold competitive national elections. Leadership selection occurs within the Chinese Communist Party through internal processes rather than popular vote. Local village elections exist in limited contexts, but they do not determine national leadership or policy direction. Representation is framed in terms of performance and responsiveness rather than electoral choice. Citizens may express grievances through petitions, online platforms, or local channels, yet these mechanisms operate under strict supervision. Comparative scholars describe this arrangement as performance-based representation, in which accountability flows upward within the party rather than outward to voters.[9]

Across these cases, electoral rules determine who gains a political voice and how that voice is translated into authority. In the United Kingdom, majoritarian rules promote stability but limit proportional representation. In Mexico and Nigeria, electoral systems aim to broaden inclusion but operate within environments

---

[7] Mohammad Ali Kadivar and Vahid Abedini, "Electoral Activism in Iran: A Mechanism for Political Change," *Comparative Politics* 52, no. 3 (2020), 1–3, 8–10, 15–17

[8] See Appendix A, Table A4

[9] Andrea Kendall-Taylor, Erica Frantz, and Joseph Wright, "The Digital Dictators: How Technology Strengthens Autocracy," *Foreign Affairs* (2020)

that challenge fairness and effectiveness. In Russia and Iran, elections exist but are carefully managed, reducing their capacity to translate voter preferences into policy. In China, elections are largely absent at the national level, and representation is defined by state performance rather than popular choice.

Elections, then, are not merely events but institutional systems that shape political outcomes. They influence whether citizens can remove leaders, whether opposition parties can grow, and whether government decisions reflect public preferences. Studying electoral systems reveals why some countries experience peaceful transitions of power, why others rely on managed participation, and why some maintain stability without competitive elections at all. Representation is never automatic. It depends on the rules that convert participation into power and determine whose voices ultimately matter.

Further Reading for Teachers

The following scholarly sources deepen the analysis of electoral systems, representation, and managed competition across democratic and authoritarian contexts.

Arowosegbe, Jeremiah O. "Nigeria at Sixty: A Failure That Succeeded." *Journal of the Historical Society of Nigeria* 29 (2020): 1–20.
Provides context for electoral participation and representation in Nigeria.

Claassen, Christopher. "Does Public Support Help Democracy Survive?" *American Journal of Political Science* 64, no. 1 (2020): 118–134.
Links electoral trust to regime stability and democratic endurance.

Kadivar, Mohammad Ali, and Vahid Abedini. "Electoral Activism in Iran." *Comparative Politics* 52, no. 3 (2020): 395–418.
Explores participation and frustration in restricted electoral systems.

Kendall-Taylor, Andrea, Erica Frantz, and Joseph Wright. "The Digital Dictators." *Foreign Affairs* 99, no. 2 (2020): 103–15.
Analyzes how authoritarian regimes manage elections and political competition.

Zagrebina, Anna. "Concepts of Democracy in Democratic and Nondemocratic Countries." *International Political Science Review* 41, no. 4 (2020): 482–498.
Useful for understanding how citizens interpret elections under different regime types.

Essay 4 Bibliography

Arowosegbe, Jeremiah O. "Nigeria at Sixty: A Failure That Succeeded." *Journal of the Historical Society of Nigeria* 29 (2020): 1–20.

Claassen, Christopher. *Does Public Support Help Democracy Survive?* Manuscript, 2019, https://www.chrisclaassen.com/docs/Claassen_democracy_public_support.pdf

Freedom House. *Freedom in the World 2023: Marking 50 Years in the Struggle for Democracy.* Washington, DC: Freedom House, 2023.

Kadivar, Mohammad Ali, and Vahid Abedini. "Electoral Activism in Iran." *Comparative Politics* 52, no. 3 (2020): 395–418.

Kendall-Taylor, Andrea, Erica Frantz, and Joseph Wright. "The Digital Dictators: How Technology Strengthens Autocracy." *Foreign Affairs*, vol. 99, no. 2, 2020, pp. 103–115.

Wood, Ethel. *AP Comparative Government & Politics: An Essential Coursebook.* 6th ed. New York: WoodYard Publications, 2013.

Essay 5
Economic Liberalization and Its Political Consequences

Economic liberalization refers to policies that reduce state control over markets, expand private enterprise, and integrate national economies into global trade and investment networks. These reforms are often justified on economic grounds, promising efficiency, growth, and modernization. Yet liberalization reshapes political life as much as economic outcomes. It alters the relationship between citizens and the state, affects perceptions of government responsibility, and redistributes power among social groups. As a result, similar economic reforms can strengthen legitimacy in one country while undermining it in another, depending on institutional strength, social inequality, and state capacity.

China provides one of the clearest examples of economic liberalization occurring alongside sustained political control. Beginning in the late 1970s, the state introduced market reforms that encouraged private enterprise, foreign investment, and export-led growth while maintaining one-party rule. These reforms generated rapid economic expansion, lifted hundreds of millions out of poverty, and transformed China into a major global economic power. World Bank data show steady increases in GDP per capita over the reform period,[1] reinforcing assessments of state economic performance and administrative effectiveness.[2] Economic success strengthened regime legitimacy, allowing the government to justify political restrictions as necessary for stability

---

[1] See Appendix B, Table B3, "Environmental Stress and Governance Capacity"

[2] World Bank, *Worldwide Governance Indicators:* "1980–2020" (Washington, DC: World Bank Group, 2023)

and development. At the same time, liberalization produced inequality, regional disparities, and environmental stress. The state has responded by tightly regulating labor organizations, information flows, and civil society, ensuring that economic openness does not translate into political pluralism. Comparative scholarship on authoritarian resilience emphasizes that performance-based legitimacy allows regimes like China's to absorb market reforms without loosening political control.[3]

Russia followed a markedly different trajectory. After the collapse of the Soviet Union, rapid liberalization and privatization in the 1990s dismantled state ownership but produced severe social disruption. Many citizens experienced unemployment, inflation, and declining living standards, while a small group of oligarchs accumulated vast wealth. Public disillusionment with market reform weakened trust in democratic institutions. Under Vladimir Putin, the state reasserted control over strategic industries, limited competition, and re-centralized political authority. Although market mechanisms remain, political power has become increasingly concentrated. Freedom House documents declining political rights and civil liberties in Russia, noting that economic stability has coincided with reduced political accountability.[4] In this case, liberalization did not lead to political openness; instead, early economic dislocation created conditions under which centralized authority regained legitimacy. Across cases, economic liberalization reshapes state–society relations in different ways, strengthening legitimacy where the state retains capacity and undermining it where reforms outpace governance.[5]

---

[3] Kendall-Taylor, Frantz, and Wright, "Digital Dictators."

[4] Freedom House, *Freedom in the World 2023: Marking 50 Years in the Struggle for Democracy* (Washington, DC: Freedom House, 2023), 1109–1116

[5] See Appendix A, Table A5, "Economic Liberalization and State Capacity Matrix"

Iran presents a more constrained and unstable interaction between liberalization and politics. The state retains control over key sectors, particularly energy, while sanctions, inflation, and unemployment limit economic growth. Young people face restricted employment opportunities, intensifying social frustration. Efforts to liberalize or attract investment are shaped by concerns about foreign influence and regime survival. Economic hardship frequently becomes a catalyst for protest, linking material grievances to demands for political reform. Demographic pressure compounds these tensions, as Iran's youthful population structure places sustained strain on labor markets and state capacity.[6] Comparative studies of protest politics in Iran show that economic stress often sharpens contention between society and the state rather than producing stable political reform, especially when political institutions block meaningful change.[7]

Comparative research suggests that economic liberalization can support democratization when accompanied by institutional reform, but it may also intensify political grievances when governance capacity remains uneven.[8] Research on democratic survival further indicates that institutional change strengthens democracy only when it produces sustained public support, helping explain why liberalization alone has not resolved Mexico's legitimacy challenges.[9]

Nigeria demonstrates the difficulty of pursuing liberalization in a context of institutional fragility and resource

---

[6] United Nations, Department of Economic and Social Affairs, Population Division, *World Population Prospects 2022: Summary of Results* (New York: United Nations, 2022), 22

[7] Mohammad Ali Kadivar and Vahid Abedini, "Electoral Activism in Iran: A Mechanism for Political Change," *Comparative Politics* 52, no. 3 (2020), 12–14, 15–17, 18–19

[8] Ethel Wood, *AP Comparative Government & Politics: An Essential Coursebook* (New York: WoodYard Publications, 2013), 72–76, 78–80

[9] Christopher Claassen, *Does Public Support Help Democracy Survive?* (unpublished manuscript, 2019), 1–2, 26–27

dependence. Market reforms, particularly in the oil sector, have been inconsistent and vulnerable to corruption. Dependence on oil revenue exposes the state to global price fluctuations, weakening fiscal stability and public service provision. High youth unemployment and regional inequality amplify political frustration, especially when reforms fail to produce inclusive growth. World Bank governance indicators highlight how weak state capacity and administrative constraints reduce the effectiveness of economic reform.[10] In Nigeria, liberalization operates within a political environment marked by weak institutions, making economic reform as likely to generate protest as legitimacy.

The United Kingdom provides a contrasting example of how strong institutions shape political responses to liberalization. Economic reforms beginning in the 1980s shifted the economy away from heavy industry toward services and finance. These changes increased efficiency and growth but also produced long-term regional and social inequalities. Deindustrialization weakened traditional labor bases, reshaped political coalitions, and intensified debates over welfare, public investment, and national identity. Even in a stable democracy, liberalization altered patterns of representation and voter behavior. Political consequences emerged not simply from national economic performance but from how different communities experienced economic change. Institutional stability allowed the system to absorb these tensions without threatening democratic continuity, but distributional effects remain central to political conflict.

Across all six cases, economic liberalization reshapes politics by redefining expectations of the state. When reforms deliver broad and visible benefits, governments gain legitimacy and public trust. When they deepen inequality, disrupt livelihoods, or expose institutional weakness, political confidence declines and

---

[10] World Bank, *Worldwide Governance Indicators*; Appendix B, Table B2. "Demographic Pressures and Population Structure"

movements for change gain momentum. Liberalization can reinforce authoritarian control, support democratic transition, or produce unstable hybrid outcomes depending on how reforms intersect with institutions, social cleavages, and state capacity. Across regimes, the political consequences of economic liberalization depend largely on whether state capacity is strong enough to manage reform, explaining why similar policies produce stability in some cases and backlash in others.[11]

Economic policy, therefore, is never merely economic. It determines whose interests are prioritized, how responsibility is allocated between state and market, and whether citizens view the political system as responsive or indifferent. Understanding liberalization is essential not only for explaining economic outcomes but for anticipating political stability, legitimacy, and change across different regimes.

---

[11] See Appendix A, Table A5

Further Reading for Teachers

The following scholarly sources deepen understanding of the political consequences of economic liberalization and are well-suited for teacher enrichment or advanced classroom discussion.

Claassen, Christopher. "Does Public Support Help Democracy Survive?" *American Journal of Political Science* 64, no. 1 (2020): 118–134.
Explores how economic satisfaction and political trust interact across regime types.

Commander, Simon, and Stavros Poupakis. "The Political Economy of Reform." IZA Institute of Labor Economics Discussion Paper, 2020.
Provides comparative insight into reform outcomes in transitional and developing economies.

Kadivar, Mohammad Ali, and Vahid Abedini. "Electoral Activism in Iran." *Comparative Politics* 52, no. 3 (2020): 395–418.
Links economic pressure, participation, and protest in constrained political systems.

Kendall-Taylor, Andrea, Erica Frantz, and Joseph Wright. "The Digital Dictators." *Foreign Affairs* 99, no. 2 (2020): 103–15.
Useful for understanding how authoritarian regimes combine economic openness with political control.

Essay 5 Bibliography

Claassen, Christopher. *Does Public Support Help Democracy Survive?* Manuscript, 2019, https://www.chrisclaassen.com/docs/Claassen_democracy_public_support.pdf

Freedom House. *Freedom in the World 2023: Marking 50 Years in the Struggle for Democracy*. Washington, DC: Freedom House, 2023.

Kadivar, Mohammad Ali, and Vahid Abedini. "Electoral Activism in Iran." *Comparative Politics* 52, no. 3 (2020): 395–418.

Kendall-Taylor, Andrea, Erica Frantz, and Joseph Wright. "The Digital Dictators: How Technology Strengthens Autocracy." *Foreign Affairs*, February 6, 2020. Author PDF, Internet Archive. https://archive.org/details/The-Digital-Dictators-How-Technology-Strengthens-Autocracy

United Nations, Department of Economic and Social Affairs, Population Division. *World Population Prospects 2022: Summary of Results*. New York: United Nations, 2022. https://www.un.org/development/desa/pd/content/World-Population-Prospects-2022.

Wood, Ethel. *AP Comparative Government & Politics: An Essential Coursebook*. 6th ed. New York: WoodYard Publications, 2013.

World Bank. *World Development Indicators*. Washington, DC: World Bank Group. https://databank.worldbank.org/source/world-development-indicators.

World Bank. *Worldwide Governance Indicators*. Washington, DC: World Bank Group, 2023. https://www.worldbank.org/en/publication/worldwide-governance-indicators.

Essay 6
Why Countries Change: Revolutions, Reforms, and Gradual Transitions

Political systems change in different ways and at different speeds. Some are transformed suddenly through revolutions that overthrow regimes, rewrite constitutions, and reshape political identities. Others evolve through reform, adjusting policies and institutions while preserving core structures. Still others experience long, uneven transitions shaped by demographics, economic pressure, social mobilization, and shifting public expectations. Understanding why countries change requires looking beyond single events to the interaction of institutions, legitimacy, state capacity, and societal forces. Political development is rarely linear, and similar pressures can produce very different outcomes across countries.

China illustrates how gradual and tightly managed change can serve state priorities. Following the upheavals of the mid-twentieth century, the government pursued economic reforms that opened markets, encouraged private enterprise, and integrated the country into the global economy while preserving one-party rule. These reforms produced sustained economic growth, rising life expectancy, and dramatic reductions in poverty. World Bank indicators document steady increases in GDP per capita alongside improvements in key social outcomes over the reform era.[1] Economic success strengthened regime legitimacy and reduced pressure for abrupt political change. Rather than liberalizing politically, the state adapted institutions to maintain control amid modernization, urbanization, and demographic transition. Change

---

[1] World Bank, *Worldwide Governance Indicators* (Washington, DC: World Bank Group, 2023); See Appendix B, Table B3, "Environmental Stress and Governance Capacity"

occurred, but it was incremental, selective, and directed from above.

Russia demonstrates how political change can reverse direction. The collapse of the Soviet Union initiated a rapid transition marked by constitutional reform, competitive elections, and expanded civil liberties. Yet weak institutions, economic dislocation, and declining living standards in the 1990s eroded public trust in democratic governance. As political authority reconsolidated under Vladimir Putin, the state reasserted control over the regions, restricted opposition activity, and brought strategic economic sectors under tighter state influence. Freedom House now classifies Russia as "Not Free," citing limited political competition and reduced civil liberties.[2] Russia's experience shows how instability and institutional weakness can lead societies to accept recentralization as a source of order, even at the expense of democratic accountability.

Iran's trajectory reflects a blend of revolutionary rupture and incremental change. The 1979 revolution replaced a monarchy with an Islamic Republic that fused religious authority with republican institutions. Since then, political evolution has occurred through elections, public debate, and periodic reform movements rather than wholesale institutional replacement. Demographic pressure plays a central role. A large proportion of Iran's population is young, and younger citizens frequently demand expanded rights, economic opportunity, and social reform. United Nations data highlight the persistence of Iran's youthful demographic structure,[3] creating sustained generational pressure on political and economic institutions.[4] At the same time,

---

[2] Freedom House, *Freedom in the World 2023: Marking 50 Years in the Struggle for Democracy* (Washington, DC: Freedom House, 2023), 1109–1116, 1487–1489
[3] See Appendix B, Table B1, "Economic Liberalization and State Capacity"
[4] United Nations, Department of Economic and Social Affairs, Population Division, *World Population Prospects 2022: Summary of Results* (New York: United Nations, 2022), 22

unelected institutions such as the Supreme Leader and the Guardian Council retain decisive power, limiting the scope of reform. Iran's political change is neither linear nor predictable, shaped by tension between popular demands and entrenched institutional authority. The divergent paths of political change— reversal, reform, and controlled adaptation—are mapped comparatively in the institutional resilience and pressure matrices.[5]

Mexico provides an example of gradual transition driven by institutional reform rather than revolution. For much of the twentieth century, one party dominated political life through a combination of electoral control, patronage, and centralized authority. Beginning in the late 1980s, economic liberalization, civil society activism, and electoral reforms expanded political competition and weakened one-party dominance. The peaceful alternation of power in 2000 marked a critical milestone in Mexico's democratization. As Ethel Wood notes, this transition reflects gradual institutional change and shifting public expectations over time rather than a single decisive political rupture.[6] Yet democratization remains incomplete. Organized crime, corruption, and regional inequality continue to constrain governance, demonstrating how transitions can advance and stall simultaneously.

Nigeria highlights how political change unfolds within the limits of state capacity. After decades of military rule, the country returned to civilian controlled government in 1999. Competitive elections, constitutional federalism, and active civil society groups support democratic practices, yet persistent violence, corruption, and economic inequality undermine institutional effectiveness. World Bank governance indicators show ongoing challenges in

---

[5] See Appendix A, *Comparative Political and Institutional Frameworks*
[6] Ethel Wood, *AP Comparative Government & Politics: An Essential Coursebook* (New York: WoodYard Publications, 2013), 67–70

governance quality and public-service delivery in Nigeria,[7] limiting the effective functioning of democratic institutions.[8] Nigeria's experience underscores that elections alone do not secure democratic consolidation. Without capable institutions and reliable governance, political transitions remain fragile and vulnerable to reversal.

The United Kingdom demonstrates how stable democracies adapt without institutional rupture. Political change occurs through elections, party realignment, judicial interpretation, and gradual policy shifts rather than revolution. Debates over national identity, regional autonomy, and economic policy continue to reshape political life, yet institutional continuity provides a framework for peaceful adjustment. Even transformative moments such as Brexit unfolded through established constitutional procedures rather than revolutionary action. The British case illustrates how a strict rule of law and trusted processes allow political systems to absorb pressure while maintaining stability.

Across all six countries, political change emerges from the interaction of social forces, economic conditions, institutional design, and public expectations. Youth bulges intensify demands for participation in Iran and Nigeria. Economic shocks destabilized Russia's post-Soviet transition. Strong state capacity has allowed China to guide change gradually and selectively. Electoral reform opened new pathways for competition in Mexico. Institutional continuity has enabled the United Kingdom to manage change without systemic disruption. These cases demonstrate that revolutions, reforms, and gradual transitions exist along a spectrum rather than as distinct categories. These trajectories of revolution, reform, and gradual transition are shaped

---

[7] See Appendix B, Table B2, "Demographic Pressures and Population Structure"

[8] World Bank, *Worldwide Governance Indicators*.

by underlying demographic pressures and institutional constraints, which help explain why political change accelerates in some cases and stalls or reverses in others.[9]

Revolutions can create new institutions but often carry high costs and uncertainty. Reforms can strengthen systems while leaving deeper tensions unresolved. Gradual transitions can build resilience but may frustrate societies seeking faster change. Understanding these pathways helps explain why countries respond differently to similar pressures and why political development rarely follows a straight line. Change is shaped not only by demands from below but by the capacity and choices of institutions that mediate those demands.

---

[9] See Appendix B, *Comparative Indicators and Structural Pressures*

Further Reading for Teachers

The following scholarly sources deepen understanding of political change, regime transition, and reform across democratic and authoritarian contexts.

Arowosegbe, Jeremiah O. "Nigeria at Sixty: A Failure That Succeeded." *Journal of the Historical Society of Nigeria* 29 (2020): 1–20.
Provides historical context for Nigeria's political transitions and institutional challenges.

Claassen, Christopher. "Does Public Support Help Democracy Survive?" *American Journal of Political Science* 64, no. 1 (2020): 118–134.
Explores how public trust influences regime stability during periods of change.

Kadivar, Mohammad Ali, and Vahid Abedini. "Electoral Activism in Iran." *Comparative Politics* 52, no. 3 (2020): 395–418.
Examines cycles of reform, participation, and institutional constraint in Iran.

Kendall-Taylor, Andrea, Erica Frantz, and Joseph Wright. "The Digital Dictators." *Foreign Affairs* 99, no. 2 (2020): 103–15.
Analyzes how authoritarian regimes adapt to social and economic change while retaining control.

Zagrebina, Anna. "Concepts of Democracy in Democratic and Nondemocratic Countries." *International Political Science Review* 41, no. 4 (2020): 482–498.
Useful for comparing how citizens interpret political change across regime types.

Essay 6 Bibliography

Freedom House. *Freedom in the World 2023: Marking 50 Years in the Struggle for Democracy*. Washington, DC: Freedom House, 2023.

United Nations, Department of Economic and Social Affairs, Population Division. *World Population Prospects 2022: Summary of Results*. New York: United Nations, 2022. https://www.un.org/development/desa/pd/content/World-Population-Prospects-2022.

Wood, Ethel. *AP Comparative Government & Politics: An Essential Coursebook*. 6th ed. New York: WoodYard Publications, 2013.

World Bank. *World Development Indicators*. Washington, DC: World Bank Group. https://databank.worldbank.org/source/world-development-indicators.

World Bank. *Worldwide Governance Indicators*. Washington, DC: World Bank Group, 2023. https://www.worldbank.org/en/publication/worldwide-governance-indicators.

Essay 7

Demographics and Destiny:
How Population Shapes Policy and Politics

Demographic change shapes political life as deeply as constitutions, elections, or economic policy. Population growth, aging, migration, and urbanization alter the relationship between citizens and the state by influencing public spending, labor markets, electoral behavior, and social stability. While demographic trends unfold gradually, their political consequences can be abrupt. A large cohort entering the labor force, a shrinking tax base supporting retirees, or rapid urban growth can strain institutions and reshape political priorities. Across the six countries examined here, demographic forces consistently define the pressures under which political systems operate.

China's demographic trajectory is dominated by rapid aging and long-term population imbalance. Decades of low fertility following the one-child policy sharply reduced population growth and accelerated the rise in median age. United Nations data show a declining working-age population alongside a growing elderly cohort in China,[1] creating sustained demographic pressures on economic growth, pension systems, and healthcare provision.[2] These demographic realities reinforce the government's emphasis on stability, productivity, and performance legitimacy. Slower growth risks undermining public confidence, prompting policy efforts to encourage higher birth rates and delay retirement. Yet high living costs, competitive education systems, and changing social expectations limit the effectiveness of these measures.

---

[1] See Appendix B, Table B4

[2] United Nations, Department of Economic and Social Affairs, Population Division, *World Population Prospects 2022: Summary of Results* (New York: United Nations, 2022), 18

Demography thus constrains policy options even in a system with strong state capacity.

Russia faces a different but equally consequential demographic challenge: sustained population decline. Low fertility, high mortality rates among working-age men, and limited net migration have produced negative population growth for decades. United Nations projections indicate continued population decline in Russia, reflecting long-term demographic contraction and negative natural increase.[3] These trends raise concerns about labor shortages, military readiness, and long-term economic capacity. The state has responded with financial incentives for families and pro-natalist rhetoric, framing demographic recovery as a matter of national strength. Politically, population decline reinforces centralized authority, as leaders prioritize cohesion and control in the face of long-term structural vulnerability.

Iran presents one of the most pronounced youth bulges among the six cases. A large share of the population is under thirty, shaped in part by high post-revolutionary birth rates. This demographic structure places intense pressure on the state to provide employment, housing, and educational opportunities. When economic performance falters or political restrictions limit opportunity, young people become a primary source of protest and reform movements. United Nations data indicate that Iran's youthful population structure places sustained demographic pressure on labor markets and state institutions.[4] Demography amplifies political demand, accelerating pressure for change even when institutions resist reform.

Nigeria's demographic profile is defined by rapid population growth and a dominant youth majority. The country is projected to become one of the world's most populous states

---

[3] United Nations, *World Population Prospects 2022*, 16

[4] United Nations, *World Population Prospects 2022*, 22; See Appendix B, Table B1

within this century. World Bank indicators highlight high fertility rates and rapid urbanization in Nigeria,[5] both of which place sustained pressure on education systems, infrastructure, housing, and employment markets.[6] A youthful population can energize political participation, but when economic opportunity and public services lag behind population growth, frustration intensifies. Youth-led movements such as #EndSARS reflect the political consequences of unmet demographic demand. Nigeria's long-term stability depends heavily on whether state capacity can keep pace with demographic expansion. Youth bulges, aging populations, and dependency pressures across the six cases are compared directly in the demographic indicators table.[7]

Mexico occupies a middle position in the demographic spectrum. Fertility rates have declined, yet the population remains relatively young compared to aging societies in Europe or East Asia. Rapid urbanization continues to reshape social and political life, concentrating populations in metropolitan areas where demands for employment, public safety, and services are most visible. Demographic change influences migration patterns, both internal and international, and shapes political priorities around development, education, and anti-corruption efforts. Compared to Nigeria or Iran, demographic pressure is less acute, but it still interacts with inequality and institutional capacity to influence political behavior.

The United Kingdom faces demographic challenges typical of advanced industrial democracies. An aging population increases demand for pensions, healthcare, and long-term care, while slower population growth raises concerns about productivity and labor supply. United Nations data show a rising median age and

---

[5] See Appendix B, Table B1, "Economic Liberalization and State Capacity"
[6] World Bank, *World Development Indicators*.
[7] See Appendix A, Table A6, "Demographics Matrix"

increasing dependency ratios in the United Kingdom,[8] reflecting ongoing population aging.[9] These trends shape electoral politics. Older voters tend to prioritize stability, healthcare, and economic security, while younger generations focus on housing affordability, climate change, and social justice. Immigration policy becomes a central political issue as governments seek to balance labor needs with public concern over social cohesion. Demography thus contributes to generational divides that increasingly define political competition.

Across all six countries, demographic pressures shape politics by defining what governments must deliver and what citizens expect. Aging societies require robust welfare systems and fiscal sustainability. Youth-heavy populations demand employment, mobility, and inclusion. Urbanization concentrates political pressure and accelerates mobilization. Population decline forces states to rethink economic strategy, family policy, and migration. Demography does not determine political outcomes on its own, but it establishes the boundaries within which policy choices are made.

Demographic change unfolds slowly, yet its political effects accumulate over time. A generation raised amid unemployment may distrust institutions. A growing urban population may demand improved infrastructure and accountability. An aging electorate may prioritize security over reform. Governments respond according to their capacity, legitimacy, and institutional design. When demographic realities align with political strategy, stability increases. When they diverge, pressure for reform or disruption intensifies. Viewed comparatively, population pressure influences politics by

---

[8] See Appendix B, Table B2, "Demographic Pressures and Population Structure"
[9] United Nations, *World Population Prospects 2022*, 18

amplifying demands on employment, services, and representation, with consequences that vary according to state capacity.[10]

Political systems that understand and anticipate demographic change are better positioned to manage the future. Those that ignore it risk being overtaken by forces that reshape politics regardless of institutional intent. Demography does not dictate destiny, but it powerfully constrains and channels political possibility.

---

[10] Appendix A, Table A6

Further Reading for Teachers

The following scholarly works deepen understanding of how demographic change influences political stability, participation, and policy across regime types.

Bloom, David E., David Canning, and Jaypee Sevilla. *The Demographic Dividend: A New Perspective on the Economic Consequences of Population Change*. Santa Monica, CA: RAND Corporation, 2003.
A foundational work on how age structure influences economic and political outcomes.

Cincotta, Richard P. *Half a Chance: Youth Bulges and Transitions to Liberal Democracy*. Washington, DC: Environmental Change and Security Program, 2008.
Useful for understanding youth pressure in cases such as Iran and Nigeria.

Urdal, Henrik. "A Clash of Generations? Youth Bulges and Political Violence." *International Studies Quarterly* 50, no. 3 (2006): 607–629.

Zagrebina, Anna. "Concepts of Democracy in Democratic and Nondemocratic Countries." *International Political Science Review* 41, no. 4 (2020): 482–498.
Helpful for linking demographic expectations to political attitudes.

Essay 7 Bibliography

United Nations, Department of Economic and Social Affairs, Population Division. *World Population Prospects 2022: Summary of Results*. New York: United Nations, 2022. https://www.un.org/development/desa/pd/content/World-Population-Prospects-2022.

World Bank. *World Development Indicators*. Washington, DC: World Bank Group. https://databank.worldbank.org/source/world-development-indicators.

World Bank. *Worldwide Governance Indicators*. Washington, DC: World Bank Group, 2023. https://www.worldbank.org/en/publication/worldwide-governance-indicators.

Environmental Crisis as
a Test of State Capacity

Environmental crises reveal the strengths and weaknesses of political systems more clearly than almost any other policy challenge. Pollution, climate change, deforestation, water scarcity, and resource degradation demand coordinated, long-term government action. These problems are scientifically complex, politically costly, and often slow to produce visible benefits. A state that manages them effectively demonstrates administrative capacity, legitimacy, and responsiveness. A state that fails exposes gaps in governance, accountability, and public trust. Across the six countries examined in this book, environmental challenges function as tests of state capacity and political priorities.

China faces some of the most severe environmental pressures resulting from decades of rapid industrialization. Air pollution, water contamination, soil degradation, and rising carbon emissions have become prominent public concerns. World Bank indicators document historically high levels of particulate matter in major Chinese cities,[1] though recent years show measurable improvement following stricter regulation and enforcement.[2] Environmental degradation has generated localized protests, particularly around air quality and water access, pushing the government to respond. China now invests heavily in renewable energy, electric transportation, and emission controls while simultaneously maintaining reliance on coal to support economic growth. The state's capacity to mobilize resources, coordinate policy, and enforce regulations reflects strong administrative

---

[1] See Appendix B, Table B3, "Environmental Stress and Governance Capacity"
[2] World Bank, *World Development Indicators.*

authority. Yet the long-term tension between growth and sustainability remains unresolved, illustrating how even high-capacity states face structural trade-offs.

Russia's environmental challenges reflect both geography and governance. Vast territory complicates monitoring and enforcement, while heavy industry, energy extraction, and aging infrastructure contribute to pollution and ecological damage. Forest fires in Siberia, industrial waste, and oil spills in Arctic regions have intensified environmental risk. Although environmental laws exist, enforcement is uneven, and powerful economic actors often operate with limited oversight. Freedom House reports low levels of civic freedom, constraining the ability of journalists and civil society organizations to pressure the state or demand transparency.[3] Environmental crises in Russia highlight weaknesses in regulatory capacity and accountability, particularly in remote regions where central authority is difficult to project.

Iran confronts acute environmental stress driven by water scarcity, desertification, and climate change. Overuse of groundwater, dam mismanagement, and rising temperatures have intensified drought conditions and reduced agricultural productivity. Policy analyses document declining water availability and increasing climate vulnerability in Iran, particularly in rural and peripheral areas,[4] where environmental stress has intensified economic hardship and social instability.[5] These environmental pressures intersect with economic hardship, contributing to displacement, unemployment, and public frustration. Water shortages have sparked protests in multiple provinces, demonstrating how environmental degradation can accelerate

---

[3] Freedom House, *Freedom in the World 2023: Marking 50 Years in the Struggle for Democracy* (Washington, DC: Freedom House, 2023), 1109–1116
[4] See Appendix B, Table B3
[5] Eric Lob, "Iran's Water Crisis Is a Warning to Other Countries," *Carnegie Endowment for International Peace*, November 24, 2025, https://www.carnegieendowment.org/.

political tension. Although the state has introduced conservation measures, sanctions, fiscal constraints, and political fragmentation limit the effectiveness of policy responses. In Iran, environmental crisis functions not only as a technical challenge but as a catalyst for broader social unrest.

Nigeria's environmental problems are closely tied to resource extraction, population growth, and weak regulatory enforcement. Decades of oil spills in the Niger Delta have contaminated land and waterways, undermining agriculture and fisheries while fueling conflict between communities, corporations, and the state. World Bank indicators document severe air pollution and environmental degradation in Nigeria,[6] alongside elevated health risks with documented economic consequences.[7] Rapid urbanization compounds these challenges, as cities struggle with waste management, air pollution, and inadequate infrastructure. Environmental governance is often undermined by corruption, limited administrative capacity, and fragmented authority. In Nigeria, environmental crisis reinforces existing inequalities and weakens public confidence in the state, linking ecological degradation to political legitimacy and security concerns. Variations in environmental governance capacity and regulatory enforcement are summarized in the state capacity and policy performance matrices.[8]

Mexico faces environmental pressures shaped by urbanization, deforestation, water scarcity, and climate change. Air pollution in major metropolitan areas, particularly Mexico City, remains a concern despite notable improvements through targeted regulation. Northern regions experience severe water shortages, while coastal areas face stronger storms and flooding. Environmental activism has expanded, especially among younger

---

[6] See Appendix B, Table B3
[7] World Bank, *World Development Indicators.*
[8] See Appendix A, Table A7, "Environment and Capacity Matrix"

citizens concerned with climate change and sustainability. However, enforcement of environmental laws varies significantly by region, and criminal organizations operating in some areas undermine conservation efforts. Mexico's environmental challenges thus reflect broader governance issues, demonstrating how state capacity and rule of law determine whether environmental policy can be effectively implemented.

The United Kingdom confronts environmental issues characteristic of advanced industrial democracies, including greenhouse gas emissions, coastal erosion, and changing rainfall patterns. As a high-income country with strong institutions, the UK possesses the administrative tools necessary to respond. It has adopted long-term climate targets, invested in renewable energy, and aligned policy with international commitments. Public support for environmental action is relatively strong, particularly among younger voters. At the same time, debates over energy costs, regional inequality, and economic transition complicate decision-making. Environmental policy in the UK illustrates how even capable states must balance scientific evidence with political feasibility and distributional concerns.

Across all six countries, environmental crises expose the relationship between state capacity and public trust. States with strong administrative systems, such as China and the United Kingdom, can implement large-scale policies and enforce regulations, even when doing so involves political risk. Countries with weaker institutions or fragmented authority struggle to monitor conditions, regulate powerful actors, or coordinate effective responses. Environmental challenges also create openings for civil society. In Mexico, Nigeria, and Iran, environmental activism often becomes a channel for broader political expression. In Russia and China, environmental issues mobilize citizens in ways that governments monitor closely, reflecting the political sensitivity of ecological protest. These cases show that environmental policy exposes variations in administrative strength and legitimacy, shaping how effectively states respond to long-term collective problems.[9]

Environmental policy demands long-term planning, transparency, and coordination across levels of government. It requires states to integrate scientific expertise into decision-making and to communicate honestly with the public about trade-offs and risks. How a country responds to environmental crisis reveals not only its commitment to sustainability but also its deeper political character. Environmental challenges test whether governments can govern for the future rather than merely manage the present.

---

[9] See Appendix A, Table A7

Further Reading for Teachers

The following scholarly works deepen understanding of environmental governance, state capacity, and political accountability across regime types.

Aklin, Michaël, and Johannes Urpelainen. "Political Competition, Path Dependence, and the Strategy of Sustainable Energy Transitions." *American Journal of Political Science* 57, no. 3 (2013): 643–58.

Beeson, Mark. "The Coming of Environmental Authoritarianism." *Environmental Politics* 19, no. 2 (2010): 276–94.
Useful for analyzing China's capacity-driven environmental governance.

Bernauer, Thomas, and Vally Koubi. "States as Providers of Public Goods: How Does Environmental Quality Affect Political Trust?" *Comparative Political Studies* 46, no. 7 (2013): 829–60.
Explores how environmental performance shapes legitimacy and public confidence.

Harrison, Kathryn, and Lisa McIntosh Sundstrom. *Global Commons, Domestic Decisions*. Cambridge, MA: MIT Press, 2010.
Compares environmental policy capacity across democracies and authoritarian systems.

Essay 8 Bibliography

Freedom House. *Freedom in the World 2023: Marking 50 Years in the Struggle for Democracy.* Washington, DC: Freedom House, 2023.

Lob, Eric. "Iran's Water Crisis Is a Warning to Other Countries." *Carnegie Endowment for International Peace*, 24 November 025, www.carnegieendowment.org.

United Nations, Department of Economic and Social Affairs, Population Division. *World Population Prospects 2022: Summary of Results.* New York: United Nations, 2022. https://www.un.org/development/desa/pd/content/World-Population-Prospects-2022.

World Bank. *World Development Indicators.* Washington, DC: World Bank Group. https://databank.worldbank.org/source/world-development-indicators.

World Bank. *Worldwide Governance Indicators.* Washington, DC: World Bank Group, 2023. https://www.worldbank.org/en/publication/worldwide-governance-indicators.

Part III
Comparative Tables, Matrices, and Visual Summaries

Appendix A
Comparative Political and Institutional Frameworks

This appendix synthesizes cross-national patterns in legitimacy, institutions, participation, and electoral competition across the six comparative cases examined.

Table A1. Sources of Political Legitimacy Across Regime Types

This table compares the primary sources of political legitimacy across the six cases, including procedural legitimacy, performance-based legitimacy, ideological authority, and nationalist narratives. It also identifies key institutional supports and recurring challenges that shape regime stability.

Category	United Kingdom	China	Russia	Iran	Mexico	Nigeria
Sources of Legitimacy	Rule of law; elections; trusted institutions	Economic performance; nationalism	Stability; centralized authority	Religious authority; revolutionary identity	Elections; reforms; civil society	Elections; federal identity; civic energy
Threats to Legitimacy	Inequality; polarization	Inequality; aging; censorship	Corruption; repression; sanctions	Youth frustration; inflation	Crime; corruption	Insecurity; corruption
Institutional Supports	Parliament; courts; free press	CCP discipline; bureaucracy	Security services; state media	Clerical institutions	INE; courts; Congress	INEC; federal system

Table A1. Sources of Political Legitimacy Across Regime Types (continued)

Category	United Kingdom	China	Russia	Iran	Mexico	Nigeria
Citizen Trust Patterns	Moderate; high locally	High central trust; lower locally	Higher trust in the presidency	Declining youth trust	Moderate election trust	High civic interest; low institutional trust
Democratic/ Authoritarian Effects	Fully democratic	Authoritarian	Hybrid authoritarian	Theocratic hybrid	Electoral democracy	Electoral democracy (fragile)

Table A2. Institutional Configuration and Distribution of Political Power

This table summarizes executive–legislative–judicial relationships across cases, highlighting the degree of separation or fusion of powers, mechanisms of accountability, and the relative autonomy of key political institutions.

Category	United Kingdom	China	Russia	Iran	Mexico	Nigeria
Executive	Parliamentary	CCP leadership	Dominant presidency	Supreme Leader + President	Presidential	Presidential
Executive Strengths	Accountability; stability	High capacity; coordination	Strong central control	Ideological cohesion	Clear mandate; checks emerging	Federal balance
Executive Weaknesses	PM dominance	No electoral control	Weak oversight	Dual authority	Corruption	Security limits
Legislature	Bicameral; independent	NPC; controlled	Bicameral; weak autonomy	Majles; clerical oversight	Bicameral; competitive	Bicameral; moderate autonomy
Judiciary	Independent	Subordinate to the CCP	Limited independence	Clerical supervision	Strengthening	Uneven independence

Table A3. Political Participation and Civil Society Constraints

This table compares patterns of political participation and civil society activity across regime types, emphasizing the extent of civic freedom, state oversight, and the capacity of organized social actors to influence policy outcomes.

Dimension	United Kingdom	China	Russia	Iran	Mexico	Nigeria
Political Participation	High; multiple channels	Limited; state-controlled	Restricted; managed opposition	Limited; protest waves	Active; competitive	Very active; protest-driven
Civil Society Strength	Strong NGOs + independent media	Controlled, monitored	Constrained; pressured	Semi-active; restricted	Expanding NGOs; rights movements	Very active; shapes politics
Media Environment	Free press	Censored	State-controlled	Partly restricted	Pluralistic	Vibrant but uneven
Role in Accountability	Strong check on power	Limited	Very limited	Cyclical pressure	Important in reforms	Essential but inconsistent

Table A4. Electoral Competition and Representation

This table classifies electoral systems according to their level of competitiveness, inclusiveness, and representational effectiveness, distinguishing between competitive, restricted, and symbolic elections across the six cases.

Category	United Kingdom	China	Russia	Iran	Mexico	Nigeria
Election Type	FPTP; competitive	No national elections	Managed elections	Elections with vetting	Mixed PR + FPTP	Presidential + legislative
Competition Level	High	None	Low	Medium	High	Medium–High
Representation Quality	Strong but underrepresents small parties	Not applicable	Weak; dominated by the ruling party	Limited by clerical vetting	Strong; includes diverse parties	Medium; varies by region
Impact on Policy	Party-controlled agendas	CCP-set agenda	President-driven	Religious + elected influence	Congress input significant	Federal balancing

Table A5. Economic Liberalization and State Capacity Matrix

Category	United Kingdom	China	Russia	Iran	Mexico	Nigeria
Liberalization Level	Mature market economy	Market reforms under the CCP	Partly liberalized; oligarchic	Limited; sanctions restrict	Opened economy; reforms ongoing	Partial; limited by corruption
Political Effects	Inequality debates	Strengthened CCP legitimacy	Empowered executive	Protest cycles	Democratization catalyst	Weak state capacity
State Capacity	Strong	Very strong administratively	Strong but centralized	Mixed; dual structure	Medium; improving	Varies by region
Reform Challenges	Regional divides	Aging; pollution	Sanctions; stagnation	Youth expectations	Corruption; violence	Infrastructure gaps

Table A6. Demographics Matrix

Category	United Kingdom	China	Russia	Iran	Mexico	Nigeria
Population Trend	Aging	Aging + imbalance	Declining	Youth bulge	Urbanizing; moderately young	Rapid growth; large youth
Key Pressures	Pension + healthcare demands	Aging workforce; care burden	Labor shortages	Youth unemployment	Migration + inequality	Urban overcrowding
Political Impact	Generational divides	Stability concerns	Centralization	Protest cycles	Electoral realignment	High mobilization

Table A7. Environment and Capacity Matrix

Category	United Kingdom	China	Russia	Iran	Mexico	Nigeria
Environmental Stress	Climate regulation + energy transition	Severe pollution; water scarcity	Forest fires; industrial pollution	Water crisis; desertification	Urban pollution; drought	Oil spills; deforestation
State Response Capacity	High	High implementation capacity	Low–medium; enforcement uneven	Limited by sanctions & governance	Medium; varies by region	Low–medium; corruption limits
Citizen Engagement	Active environmental activism	Controlled; monitored	Limited	Rising activism among youth	Growing activism	Strong activism in affected regions

Appendix B
Comparative Indicators and Structural Pressures

This appendix summarizes key cross-national patterns referenced throughout the essays using categorical indicators derived from standard comparative datasets. The tables synthesize recurring structural pressures rather than reproduce raw data.

Table B1. Economic Liberalization and State Capacity

Sources: *World Bank, World Development Indicators; World Bank, Worldwide Governance Indicators*

Country	Level of Economic Liberalization	Administrative Capacity	Political Effect of Reform
United Kingdom	High, long-established	High	Liberalization reinforces stable democratic governance and institutional trust
China	High, state-managed	High	Sustained growth and poverty reduction without political liberalization
Iran	Limited, tightly constrained	Medium–Low	Economic pressure and grievance without durable reform outcomes
Russia	Medium, uneven	Medium	Market reform accompanied by political centralization and weak accountability
Mexico	Medium–High	Medium	Electoral competition expands, but capacity gaps limit distributive trust
Nigeria	Low–Medium	Low	Liberalization yields limited governance improvement and weak reform impact

Table B2. Demographic Pressures and Population Structure

Source: United Nations, World Population Prospects 2022

Country	Dominant Demographic Pattern	Political Pressure Generated
United Kingdom	Aging population	Rising dependency pressure; fiscal and welfare strain
China	Rapid aging; shrinking workforce	Long-term growth constraints; pension and care burdens
Iran	Large youth cohort	Protest cycles driven by unmet economic and political expectations
Russia	Population decline	Regional depopulation and uneven service provision
Mexico	Transitional (youthful → aging)	Mixed participation pressures and uneven institutional demand
Nigeria	Large youth bulge	Intense governance strain; high mobilization with low institutional absorption

Table B3. Environmental Stress and Governance Capacity

Sources: World Bank, World Development Indicators; WHO (contextual)

Country	Primary Environmental Stress	Regulatory Capacity
United Kingdom	Low–moderate pollution	High
China	High pollution, improving	High
Iran	Water scarcity and environmental degradation	Medium–Low
Russia	Industrial pollution	Medium
Mexico	Urban pollution	Medium
Nigeria	Severe pollution and environmental degradation	Low

Appendix C
Institutional Structure Diagrams

Appendix C provides a limited set of schematic diagrams illustrating the formal institutional structures of the political systems examined in this study. These figures are intended to support readers' understanding of how authority is organized, distributed, and constrained within each case, including executive–legislative relationships, electoral system design, and the presence of unelected oversight bodies. The diagrams are descriptive rather than evaluative: they do not measure legitimacy, performance, participation, or policy outcomes, all of which are addressed through empirical indicators and comparative analysis elsewhere in the text. Accordingly, Appendix C is cited selectively and sparingly, only where visual representation clarifies institutional arrangements discussed in the essays. The figures serve as structural reference tools, complementing—but not substituting for—the analytical frameworks in Appendix A or the indicator-based summaries in Appendix B.

C1. Parliamentary System (United Kingdom)

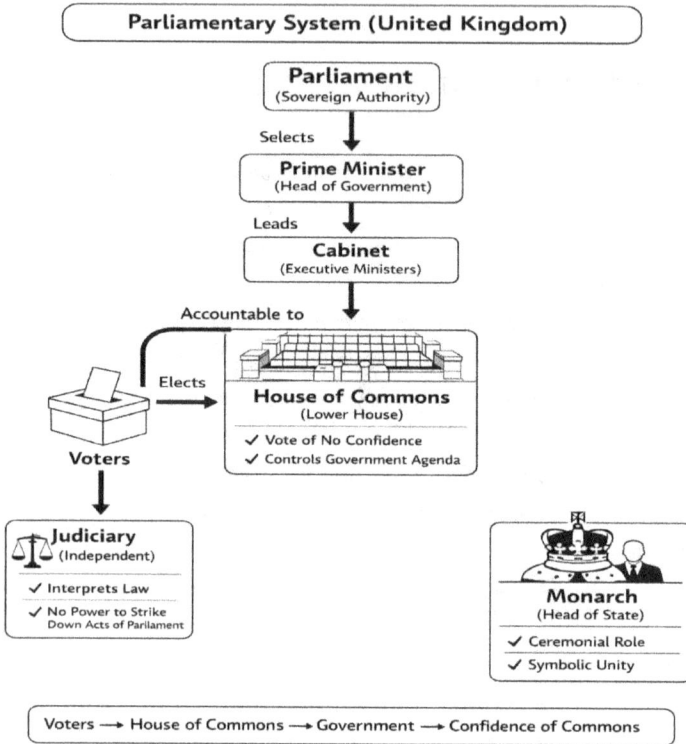

Parliamentary System (United Kingdom)

Parliament
(Sovereign Authority)

Selects

Prime Minister
(Head of Government)

Leads

Cabinet
(Executive Ministers)

Accountable to

House of Commons
(Lower House)
- ✓ Vote of No Confidence
- ✓ Controls Government Agenda

Elects

Voters

Judiciary
(Independent)
- ✓ Interprets Law
- ✓ No Power to Strike Down Acts of Parliament

Monarch
(Head of State)
- ✓ Ceremonial Role
- ✓ Symbolic Unity

Voters → House of Commons → Government → Confidence of Commons

C2. Presidential System (Mexico, Nigeria)

Presidential System (Mexico, Nigeria)

Voters

Elect separately

President
(Head of State & Government)

Legislature
(Bicameral Congress)

Appoints

Cabinet
(Executive Administration)

Judiciary
(Independent)

Legislature
(Bicameral Congress)
✓ Makes law
✓ Checks president

President
(Executive Administration)
✓ Makes law
✓ Checks president

Separate elections ⟶ Separate mandates ⟶ **Checks and balances**
⟶ Fixed presidential terms

C3. Semi-Presidential System (Russia, Iran Hybrid)

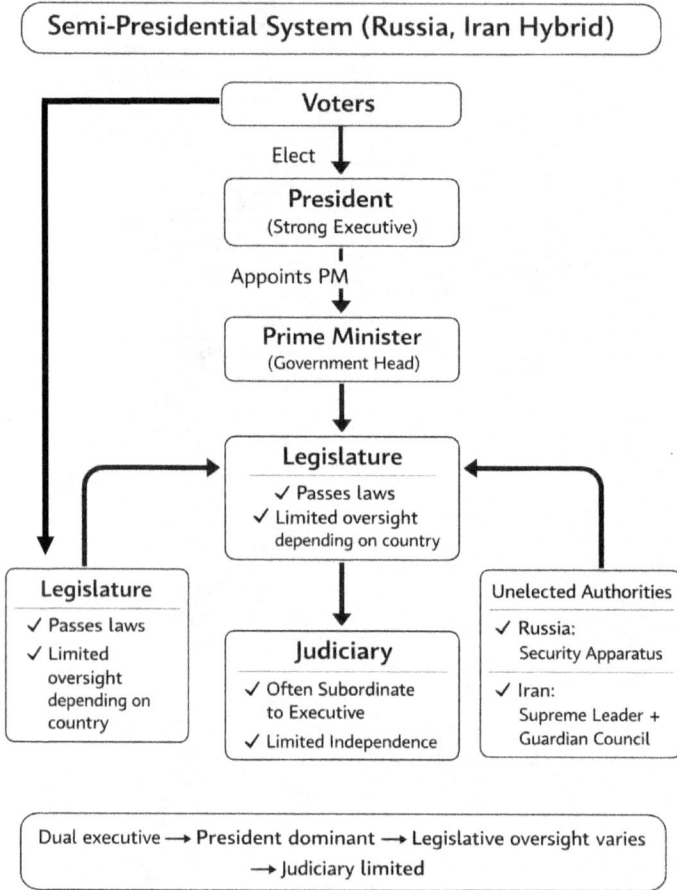

Semi-Presidential System (Russia, Iran Hybrid)

Voters

Elect ↓

President
(Strong Executive)

Appoints PM ↓

Prime Minister
(Government Head)

↓

Legislature
✓ Passes laws
✓ Limited oversight
depending on country

↓

Legislature
✓ Passes laws
✓ Limited oversight depending on country

Judiciary
✓ Often Subordinate to Executive
✓ Limited Independence

Unelected Authorities
✓ Russia:
Security Apparatus
✓ Iran:
Supreme Leader + Guardian Council

Dual executive → President dominant → Legislative oversight varies → Judiciary limited

C4. CCP-led Party-State (China)

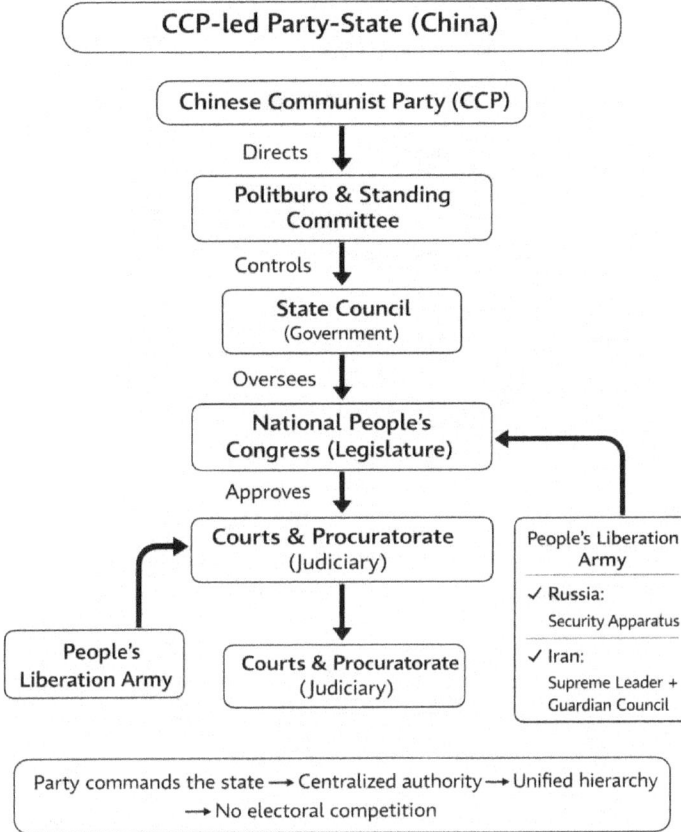

CCP-led Party-State (China)

Chinese Communist Party (CCP)

Directs ↓

Politburo & Standing Committee

Controls ↓

State Council
(Government)

Oversees ↓

National People's Congress (Legislature)

Approves ↓

Courts & Procuratorate
(Judiciary)

People's Liberation Army

✓ Russia:
Security Apparatus

✓ Iran:
Supreme Leader + Guardian Council

People's Liberation Army

Courts & Procuratorate
(Judiciary)

Party commands the state → Centralized authority → Unified hierarchy → No electoral competition

91

C5. Iran's Theocratic-Republic Hybrid

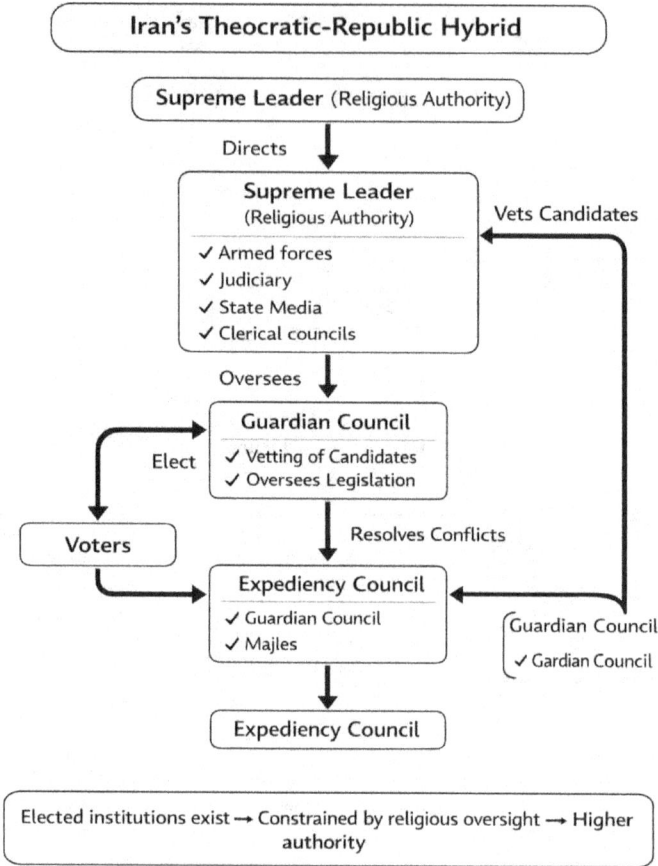

Iran's Theocratic-Republic Hybrid

Supreme Leader (Religious Authority)

Directs

Supreme Leader
(Religious Authority)

✓ Armed forces
✓ Judiciary
✓ State Media
✓ Clerical councils

Vets Candidates

Oversees

Guardian Council
✓ Vetting of Candidates
✓ Oversees Legislation

Elect

Voters

Resolves Conflicts

Expediency Council
✓ Guardian Council
✓ Majles

Guardian Council

✓ Gardian Council

Expediency Council

Elected institutions exist → Constrained by religious oversight → Higher authority

C6. Electoral Systems Diagram

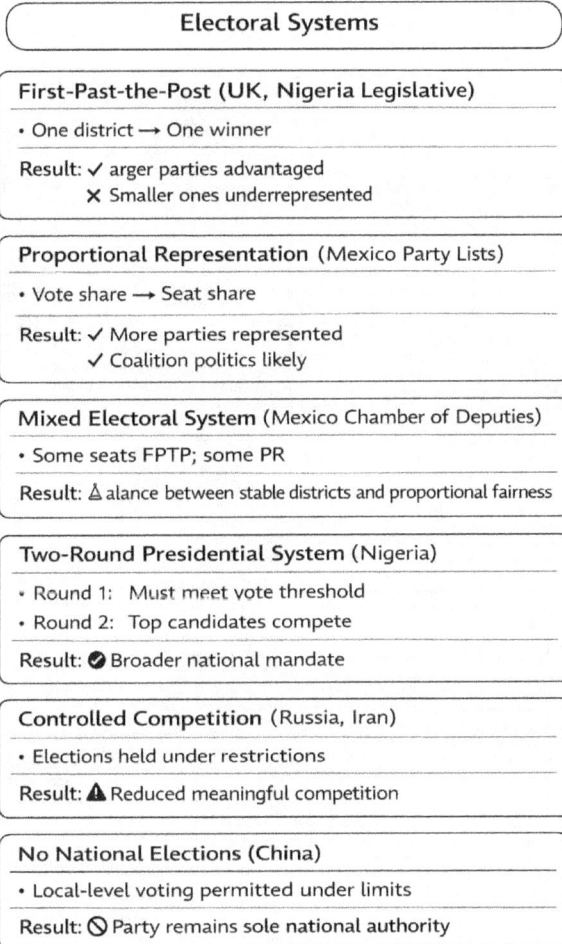

Electoral Systems

First-Past-the-Post (UK, Nigeria Legislative)

• One district ⟶ One winner

Result: ✓ arger parties advantaged
     ✗ Smaller ones underrepresented

Proportional Representation (Mexico Party Lists)

• Vote share ⟶ Seat share

Result: ✓ More parties represented
     ✓ Coalition politics likely

Mixed Electoral System (Mexico Chamber of Deputies)

• Some seats FPTP; some PR

Result: △ alance between stable districts and proportional fairness

Two-Round Presidential System (Nigeria)

• Round 1: Must meet vote threshold
• Round 2: Top candidates compete

Result: ✔ Broader national mandate

Controlled Competition (Russia, Iran)

• Elections held under restrictions

Result: ⚠ Reduced meaningful competition

No National Elections (China)

• Local-level voting permitted under limits

Result: ⊘ Party remains sole national authority

C7. Regime Type Classification Diagram

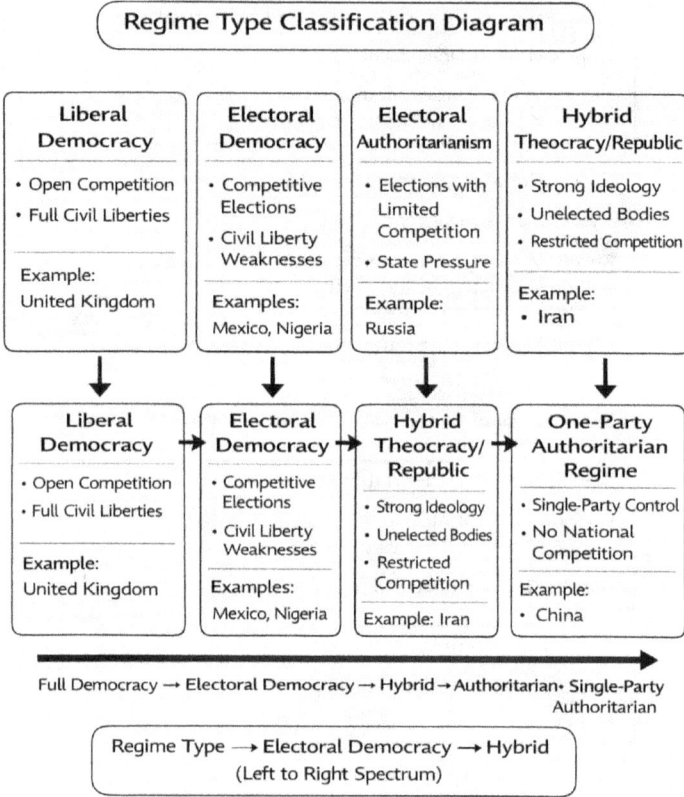

Regime Type Classification Diagram

Liberal Democracy	Electoral Democracy	Electoral Authoritarianism	Hybrid Theocracy/Republic
• Open Competition • Full Civil Liberties Example: United Kingdom	• Competitive Elections • Civil Liberty Weaknesses Examples: Mexico, Nigeria	• Elections with Limited Competition • State Pressure Example: Russia	• Strong Ideology • Unelected Bodies • Restricted Competition Example: • Iran

Liberal Democracy	Electoral Democracy	Hybrid Theocracy/ Republic	One-Party Authoritarian Regime
• Open Competition • Full Civil Liberties Example: United Kingdom	• Competitive Elections • Civil Liberty Weaknesses Examples: Mexico, Nigeria	• Strong Ideology • Unelected Bodies • Restricted Competition Example: Iran	• Single-Party Control • No National Competition Example: • China

Full Democracy → Electoral Democracy → Hybrid → Authoritarian· Single-Party Authoritarian

Regime Type → Electoral Democracy → Hybrid
(Left to Right Spectrum)

C8. Separation vs. Fusion of Powers Diagram

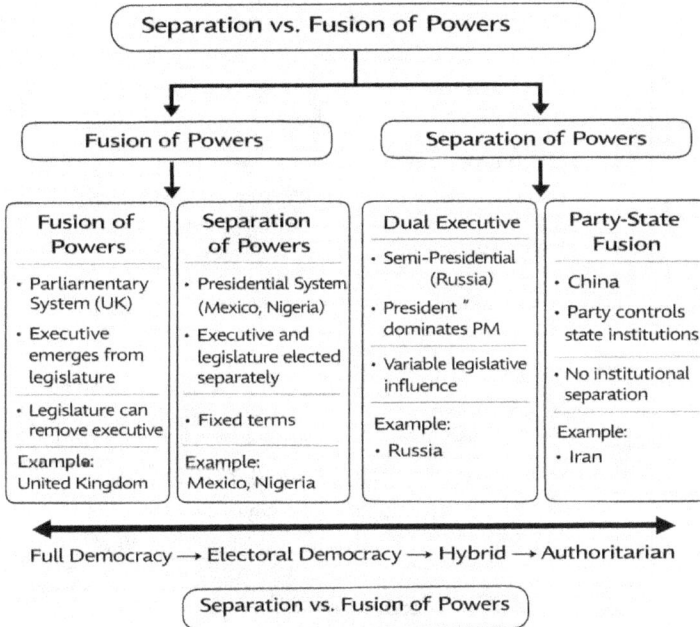

```
            ┌─────────────────────────────────────┐
            │   Separation vs. Fusion of Powers    │
            └─────────────────────────────────────┘
                             │
            ┌────────────────┴────────────────┐
            ▼                                  ▼
┌───────────────────────┐        ┌───────────────────────┐
│   Fusion of Powers    │        │  Separation of Powers │
└───────────────────────┘        └───────────────────────┘
            │                                  │
            ▼                                  ▼
```

Fusion of Powers	Separation of Powers	Dual Executive	Party-State Fusion
• Parliarnentary System (UK)	• Presidential System (Mexico, Nigeria)	• Semi-Presidential (Russia)	• China
• Executive emerges from legislature	• Executive and legislature elected separately	• President " dominates PM	• Party controls state institutions
• Legislature can remove executive		• Variable legislative influence	• No institutional separation
Cxample: United Kingdom	• Fixed terms	Example:	Example:
	Example: Mexico, Nigeria	• Russia	• Iran

◄──►

Full Democracy ⟶ Electoral Democracy ⟶ Hybrid ⟶ Authoritarian

┌─────────────────────────────────────┐
│   Separation vs. Fusion of Powers   │
└─────────────────────────────────────┘

C9. State Capacity & Accountability Diagram

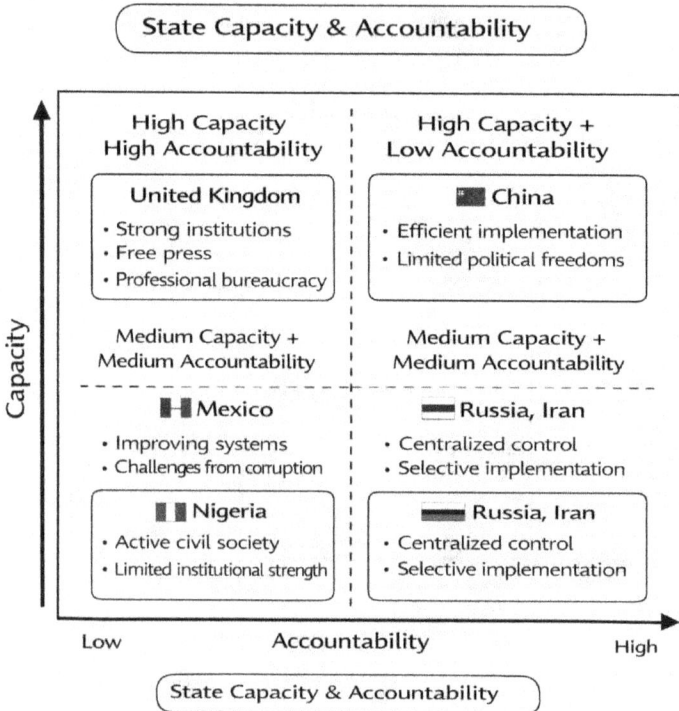

State Capacity & Accountability

High Capacity **High Accountability**	**High Capacity +** **Low Accountability**
United Kingdom • Strong institutions • Free press • Professional bureaucracy	**China** • Efficient implementation • Limited political freedoms
Medium Capacity + **Medium Accountability**	**Medium Capacity +** **Medium Accountability**
Mexico • Improving systems • Challenges from corruption	**Russia, Iran** • Centralized control • Selective implementation
Nigeria • Active civil society • Limited institutional strength	**Russia, Iran** • Centralized control • Selective implementation

Capacity

Low   Accountability   High

State Capacity & Accountability

96

Glossary of Key Comparative Terms

Accountability - Mechanisms that hold officials responsible for their actions.

Aging Population - A demographic trend where the proportion of older adults increases, influencing welfare and economic policy.

Authoritarian Regime - A system where power is concentrated in the executive and political competition and liberties are restricted.

Authoritarian Resilience - The ability of a non-democratic system to maintain control despite pressures for change.

Bureaucracy - Professional officials who carry out government functions and implement policy.

Cabinet - Senior officials who head major government departments and advise the executive.

Censorship - Government restriction of information and media.

Checks and Balances - Mechanisms that prevent any branch from dominating the political system.

Civil Liberties - Freedoms such as speech, press, protest, and religion.

Civil Rights - Legal protections against discrimination.

Civil Society - Voluntary organizations independent from the state, including NGOs, unions, charities, religious associations, and community groups.

Clientelism - A system where political support is exchanged for material benefits.

Corruption - Abuse of public office for personal gain.

Democracy - A political system with competitive elections, civil liberties, and independent institutions.

Demographic Transition - The shift from high birth and death rates to low birth and death rates.

Devolution - The transfer of power from the national government to regional or local governments.

Economic Liberalization - Reforms that open markets, reduce state control, and encourage private enterprise.

Electoral Integrity - The fairness and transparency of the electoral process.

Executive - The branch that implements laws and carries out the daily administration of the state.

Federal State - A system that divides power between national and subnational governments, each with constitutional authority.

First-Past-the-Post (FPTP) - A plurality electoral system where the candidate with the most votes wins.

Fusion of Powers - When executive and legislative branches overlap (as in parliamentary systems).

GDP per Capita - Economic output per person, used to measure development.

Globalization - Growing interconnectedness of economies, cultures, and politics.

Head of Government - The official responsible for running government policy (e.g., prime minister).

Head of State - A symbolic leader who represents the nation (e.g., monarch, president). Sometimes combined with the head of government.

Human Development Index (HDI) - A composite measure of life expectancy, education, and income.

Hybrid Regime - A system that combines formal democratic elements (such as elections) with authoritarian practices (such as media restriction).

Interest Group - An organization that seeks to influence public policy without running candidates for office.

Judicial Independence - The ability of courts to make decisions free from executive or legislative interference.

Judiciary - Courts responsible for interpreting laws and reviewing government actions.

Legislature - The law-making body of a state. It may be unicameral or bicameral.

Migration - Movement of people across borders, affecting labor markets, identity, and political debates.

Mixed Electoral System - Combines elements of FPTP and PR.

Multimember District (MMD) - A district that elects multiple representatives.

Party System - The pattern of competition among political parties (e.g., dominant-party, two-party, multiparty).

Political Culture - Shared attitudes about government, authority, and political life.

Political Participation - Ways citizens take part in political life, including voting, protesting, volunteering, or advocating online.

Political Party - An organized group that seeks political power by competing in elections.

Political Socialization - The process by which individuals learn political beliefs and values, often through family, education, media, or religion.

Political Stability - The degree to which a government and institutions remain functional and predictable.

Privatization - Transferring state-owned industries to private ownership.

Proportional Representation (PR) - Seats in the legislature are allocated based on each party's share of the vote.

Public Policy - Government actions meant to address a public issue.

Reform - Gradual change within a political system.

Regime Change - A shift in the basic rules of the political system (not just a change of leaders).

Rent-Seeking - Using political power to gain economic advantage without creating value.

Revolution - A rapid and fundamental transformation of political authority or institutions.

Rule of Law - The principle that all individuals, including government leaders, are subject to the law.

Separation of Powers - When executive, legislative, and judicial powers are held by separate branches.

Single-Member District (SMD) - An electoral district that chooses one representative.

Social Cleavages - Divisions in society based on ethnicity, religion, class, region, or language that influence political behavior.

State Capacity - The ability of a government to implement policies effectively.

Subsidy - Government financial support to industries or consumers.

Theocracy - A political system in which religious authorities hold significant governing power.

Transparency - Openness in government operations and decision making.

Two-Round System - A majoritarian system where a second election is held if no candidate wins a required threshold.

Unitary State - A system where most political authority is held by the national government.

Youth Bulge - A population with a large share of young adults, often linked to political activism or instability.

Country Profiles

A Comparative Guide to the Big Six Political Systems

United Kingdom — Country Profile

The United Kingdom is a consolidated parliamentary democracy with strong rule-of-law traditions and long-standing political institutions. Sovereignty rests with Parliament, and the executive emerges from the majority party in the House of Commons. The prime minister leads the government, while the monarch serves as a symbolic head of state. The judiciary is fully independent, with the UK Supreme Court acting as the final legal authority.

The UK maintains legitimacy through competitive elections, stable institutions, and a professional civil service. Political parties are central to representation, and citizens participate through voting, local councils, unions, advocacy groups, and a vibrant media environment. Civil society and press freedom contribute significantly to accountability.

Current challenges include regional divisions, inequality, and debates over national identity following Brexit. Despite these pressures, the UK remains a model of democratic governance. Students study the UK to understand parliamentary systems, the fusion of powers, and gradual institutional evolution.

China — Country Profile

China is an authoritarian one-party state led by the Chinese Communist Party (CCP). The political system centers on party control, with the general secretary holding the most powerful position in the country. The National People's Congress is the official legislature, but does not challenge party decisions. Courts operate under CCP authority, and the military reports to the party rather than the state.

China builds legitimacy through economic performance, nationalism, infrastructure development, and social stability.

Participation is tightly managed. Local elections exist but play a limited role. Civil society organizations operate under strict regulations, and media and online expression are censored. The CCP's authority is maintained through centralized decision-making and extensive surveillance capacity.

China faces demographic aging, economic transitions, and environmental pressures. These challenges highlight the relationship between development and political control. The country is essential for students studying authoritarian resilience, party-led governance, and state capacity.

Russia — Country Profile

Russia is a centralized, authoritarian system with limited political pluralism. The president holds dominant authority, supported by a strong security apparatus and a loyal bureaucracy. Although Russia has a multiparty structure and elections, competition is tightly managed. The State Duma and Federation Council function within constraints set by the executive. Courts lack independence and often reinforce executive priorities.

Legitimacy in Russia draws from national identity, security, and promises of stability. Media outlets operate under significant state influence, and civil society groups face legal and administrative pressure. Participation occurs, but genuine opposition has limited impact on policy outcomes.

Russia's political challenges include economic stagnation, sanctions, demographic decline, and ongoing conflicts that affect state capacity and legitimacy. Students analyze Russia to understand dominant-party rule, authoritarian centralization, and managed elections.

Iran — Country Profile

Iran operates under a theocratic republic where political authority is shared between elected offices and religious institutions. The Supreme Leader holds ultimate power, overseeing the military, judiciary, and major policy decisions. The president and parliament are elected, but candidates must be approved by the Guardian Council, which limits competition. Dual authority creates tension between ideological guidance and administrative governance.

Legitimacy comes from religious identity, revolutionary values, and national sovereignty. Citizens participate through elections, religious associations, and periodic protest movements. Civil society is active but constrained, and the media is subject to state oversight. Younger generations have increasingly challenged economic conditions, social restrictions, and political limits.

Iran faces demographic shifts, water scarcity, economic sanctions, and public demands for reform. The country helps students examine the dynamics of hybrid regimes, the role of religion in politics, and the tension between elected and unelected institutions.

Mexico — Country Profile

Mexico is a federal presidential democracy that underwent a major political transition in the late twentieth century. After decades of one-party rule by the Institutional Revolutionary Party (PRI), Mexico developed competitive elections and created strong electoral institutions. The National Electoral Institute (INE) oversees elections and maintains public confidence. Power is divided among the president, Congress, the judiciary, and state governments.

Legitimacy relies on competitive elections, institutional reform, and increasing judicial independence. Participation includes voting, activism, social movements, and a diverse media environment. Civil society is active and often challenges

103

corruption and inequality. However, violence, organized crime, and regional disparities continue to affect political trust and state capacity.

Mexico is a key case for understanding democratization, federalism, mixed electoral systems, and institutional reform. It highlights how democratic gains can coexist with persistent security challenges.

Nigeria — Country Profile

Nigeria is a federal presidential republic with significant ethnic, religious, and regional diversity. It operates an electoral democracy with recurring challenges of corruption, insecurity, and uneven state capacity. The president holds executive authority, while the National Assembly and judiciary function with varying degrees of independence. Federalism distributes power across 36 states, shaping political competition and identity.

Legitimacy depends on elections, federal representation, and the expectation that the government should manage diversity fairly. Participation is high, especially among youth and civil society groups. Media is active but faces risks in conflict regions, and civil society organizations play an important role in transparency and reform efforts.

Nigeria's main challenges include insurgency, economic inequality, infrastructure deficits, and rapid population growth. It is central to comparative politics because it illustrates the difficulties of democratization, federal governance, and political participation in a large, diverse developing state.

Notes

These notes clarify terminology and analytical assumptions used throughout the essays and accompanying diagrams. They are explanatory rather than evidentiary and are not intended as citations.

Notes for Essay 1 — What Makes Power Legitimate?
1. "Legitimacy" is used in a political-science sense: public belief that a government has the right to rule.
2. Social trust relates to—but is not the same as—legitimacy.
3. V-Dem measures referenced include the Electoral Democracy Index and the Civil Society Participation Index.
4. Freedom House scores cited refer to Political Rights and Civil Liberties.

Notes for Essay 2 — Why Political Institutions Matter
1. "Parliamentary," "presidential," and "semi-presidential" describe executive–legislative relationships.
2. Russia's structure is formally semi-presidential but functionally dominant-presidential.
3. Judicial independence is defined here as freedom from political interference and presence of institutional protections.

Notes for Essay 3 — Civil Society in Democratization and Control
1. "Civil society" includes organizations operating independently of the state, even if regulated by it.
2. Iran's restrictions combine legal vetting with informal pressure.

Notes for Essay 4 — Elections and Representation
1. "Representation quality" refers to proportionality, competitiveness, and meaningful choice.
2. China's "elections" exist only at subnational levels under CCP oversight.

Notes for Essay 5 — Economic Liberalization and Political Consequences
1. Liberalization means reducing state economic control.
2. Reform examples are simplified for instructional clarity.

Notes for Essay 6 — Why Countries Change
1. "Revolution," "reform," and "transition" follow standard comparative definitions of the pace and depth of political change.
2. Authoritarian resilience discussions rely on mainstream political-science frameworks but are presented in accessible language.

Notes for Essay 7 — Demographics and Destiny
1. Aging is defined by rising median age and declining fertility.
2. Youth bulges relate to higher mobilization but produce varied political outcomes.

Notes for Essay 8 — Environmental Crisis and State Capacity
1. Environmental indicators are drawn conceptually from UN and Our World in Data datasets.
2. "State capacity" refers to administrative and implementation capability.

Bibliography

Freedom House. *Freedom in the World 2023: Marking 50 Years in the Struggle for Democracy*. Washington, DC: Freedom House, 2023.

Fukuyama, Francis. "What Is Governance?" *Governance* 26, no. 3 (2013): 347–68.

International Institute for Democracy and Electoral Assistance (International IDEA). *Electoral System Design Database*. Stockholm: IDEA, 2023. https://www.idea.int/data-tools.

Inter-Parliamentary Union (IPU). *Parline: Global Data on National Parliaments*. Geneva: IPU, 2023. https://data.ipu.org.

Levitsky, Steven, and Lucan A. Way. *Competitive Authoritarianism: Hybrid Regimes after the Cold War*. Cambridge: Cambridge University Press, 2010.

Lijphart, Arend. *Patterns of Democracy: Government Forms and Performance in Thirty-Six Countries*. 2nd ed. New Haven, CT: Yale University Press, 2012.

Organisation for Economic Co-operation and Development (OECD). *OECD Data*. Paris: OECD, 2023. https://data.oecd.org.

Our World in Data. "Environmental Indicators." 2023. https://ourworldindata.org.

United Nations, Department of Economic and Social Affairs, Population Division. *World Population Prospects 2022: Summary of Results*. New York: United Nations, 2022. https://www.un.org/development/desa/pd/content/World-Population-Prospects-2022.

United Nations Development Programme (UNDP). *Human Development Report 2022: Uncertain Times, Unsettled Lives: Shaping Our Future in a Transforming World*. New York: United Nations, 2022. https://hdr.undp.org.

Varieties of Democracy (V-Dem) Institute. *V-Dem Dataset v.12.* University of Gothenburg, 2023. https://v-dem.net.

Weber, Max. *Economy and Society: An Outline of Interpretive Sociology.* Edited by Guenther Roth and Claus Wittich. Berkeley: University of California Press, 1978.

Wood, Ethel. *AP Comparative Government & Politics: An Essential Coursebook.* 6th ed. New York: WoodYard Publications, 2013.

World Bank. *World Development Indicators.* Washington, DC: World Bank Group. https://databank.worldbank.org/source/world-development-indicators.

World Bank. *Worldwide Governance Indicators.* Washington, DC: World Bank Group, 2023. https://www.worldbank.org/en/publication/worldwide-governance-indicators.

Index (A–Z)

Appendix references indicate locations of comparative tables and matrices summarizing cross-national patterns.

Classroom Activities

Activity 1 — The Legitimacy Debate
> Groups defend one form of legitimacy (electoral, performance, ideological, religious) and argue why it is most durable.

Activity 2 — Build-a-Regime Simulation
> Students design fictional political systems, selecting executive structure, legislature type, party system, and civil society openness.

Activity 3 — Electoral System Lab
> Using a fictional dataset, students simulate elections under FPTP, PR, and mixed systems and compare outcomes.

Activity 4 — Economic Reform Workshop
> Students evaluate political effects of reforms in China, Russia, Mexico, and Nigeria using the liberalization matrix.

Activity 5 — Why Countries Change?
> Students classify political events as reforms, revolutions, or transitions and defend their reasoning.

Activity 6 — Demographic Futures Forecast
> Students predict 20-year political trajectories for one Big Six country based on demographic data.

Activity 7 — Environmental Stress Assessment
> Students map environmental challenges and connect them to state capacity and legitimacy.

For more resources on AP Comparative Government and Politics, visit the **Mr. Hutchings History Resource Library** at www.TeachersPayTeachers.com.

www.ingramcontent.com/pod-product-compliance
Lightning Source LLC
Chambersburg PA
CBHW062101270326
41931CB00013B/3173